HISTORIC YORKSHIRE

RICHARD A. POWELL

T0322697

The History Press

*To the memory of J. H. Wardle (1923–1985), Yorkshire CCC, England
and the MCC, and to all the players and staff, past and present,
of the Yorkshire County Cricket Club.*

For *Oscar*, my great nephew, and *Betsan*, my granddaughter,
as the first representatives of the new generation of the family.

Bradford for cash,
Halifax for dash,
Wakefield for pride and poverty;
Huddersfield for show,
Sheffield's what's low,
Leeds for dirt and vulgarity.
(A nineteenth-century popular verse)

From Hull, Hell and Halifax
Good Lord, deliver us
(Attributed to the seventeenth century)

Castleford women must needs be fair
For they bathe in the Calder
And rinse in the Aire.

First published 2009

The History Press
97 St George's Place,
Cheltenham, Gloucestershire, GL50 3QB
www.thehistorypress.co.uk

British Library Cataloguing in Publication Data.
A catalogue record for this book is available from the British Library.

ISBN 978 0 7524 4926 5

Typesetting and origination by The History Press
Printed by TJ Books Limited, Padstow, Cornwall

Contents

Introduction

Historic Yorkshire is a revised, updated and combined edition of two earlier and much smaller books about the county of Yorkshire and its origins, past and traditions: *Historic Yorkshire*, originally published by Dalesman Books in 1976, and *Aspects of Yorkshire*, published in 1980. Both consisted of a short collection of essays on individual topics and themes about Yorkshire, and have been out of print for some time. These essays first appeared in print in the form of a series of magazine articles. With additional material, text and commentary, they are hereby reissued as *Historic Yorkshire*. Where necessary, the text has been amended and updated where this seems essential for accuracy, relevance and applicability.

The object of this new revised edition of the book remains the same now as it was for the original book in 1976: 'to serve as an introduction to the absorbing and fascinating story of the county of Yorkshire and its past'. The time seems right now to make these books and their contents available once more, as the interest in the White Rose County is now greater than ever before.

Any book of this nature, primarily dealing with historical themes, depends heavily on the source material and references used. Where information and details have been quoted directly or used indirectly from historical source materials, the language, style, punctuation, spelling and grammar have been kept as close as possible to those original sources. Some of these resources, and the direct and indirect quotations taken from them, might appear rather antiquated to a modern reader. For example, the conventions of punctuation, spelling and grammar are not exactly the same today as was the case in the Victorian era, or in the eighteenth century, or from even earlier times. Changes have been made only in those instances where misunderstandings might otherwise arise.

One particular difference is in the more common use of the passive voice and tense, rather than the active voice, in the literature of the last century and earlier times. Personally, I don't find this a problem but some readers, particularly those used to more modern expressions and idioms of language and literature, might have some issue with the register, style and approach. However, I contend that using the grammatical style and language as it was actually written at the time gives a more genuine and accurate sense, feel, style, tone and atmosphere to the material and the thoughts, ideas and impressions conveyed. This, I believe, makes the content and context all the more relevant, effective, lively, evocative and, most important of all, historically accurate.

When *Historic Yorkshire* first appeared, local government reorganisation had just redrawn the centuries-old boundaries of the old shires, often to the clear detriment of Yorkshire and other counties. The three Ridings of the county of Yorkshire were replaced by the administrative areas of North Yorkshire, West Yorkshire and South Yorkshire (another new invention, as there had never been a South Riding except in the novels of Winifred Holtby). The 'new' counties of Humberside and Cleveland were invented, with Cleveland replacing an earlier artificial contrivance of Teesside. Some parts of Yorkshire even ended up after reorganisation being administered by Greater Manchester or Lancashire. This could only be considered as heresy and anathema to any native-born Yorkshireman. Opposition grew to such moves by local bureaucrats and government officials. Large numbers of people in East Yorkshire were reported as refusing to use Humberside in their addresses or on their letters. The Post Office was even accused of delaying the letters and mail that refused to acknowledge and use the nomenclature of the new counties and boundaries.

These county boundary and local administration changes came about as a result of the Local Government Act 1972. Later reorganisation and further local governmental changes then took place in 1986. This time the county of West Yorkshire was divided into the five metropolitan areas and unitary authorities of Bradford, Calderdale, Kirklees, Leeds, and Wakefield. South Yorkshire was also reorganised in 1986 with Barnsley, Doncaster, Rotherham and Sheffield designated as metropolitan districts.

In more recent years, some of the reorganisation and those earlier imposed boundary changes have at last been undone. Humberside has disappeared (with the changes made in 1996) and has been replaced by the unitary authorities of the East Riding of Yorkshire, the City of Kingston upon Hull, North Lincolnshire and North East Lincolnshire. These changes have everything to do with the supposed improvements, efficiencies and consolidation of local government administration and nothing at all to do with the individual citizen's sense of local identity, history and heritage.

Yorkshire, 'God's own county', has a proud heritage and tradition. The county has its own flag with the White Rose. It has its own dish, Yorkshire pudding, truly renowned in the culinary world. The county boasts its own daily morning newspaper, the *Yorkshire Post*, which is a daily journal of genuine quality to compete with and rival the best of the national broadsheets. Yorkshire has its own regiment, its own confectionery – the Yorkshire 'humbug' – and many museums and art galleries as fine as any in the country. Of all the counties or shires in the United Kingdom, Yorkshire people can rightly be the most proud of their heritage.

Back in 1976, the BBC had enjoyed much success with the relatively new series *Last of the Summer Wine*. This series was based and filmed in real locations in Holmbridge, Holmfirth, Emley, Huddersfield and environs. The series is still hugely popular today – more than three decades later – after several changes of characters and personnel, and has rightly achieved cult status. Yorkshire's own independent television channel had *Emmerdale Farm*, later shortened to *Emmerdale*, but originally an everyday story of country folk and farming people in the Dales. *Emmerdale* has become almost a mini-industry in itself as a Yorkshire tourist attraction and feature, which is tremendous progress from the original location based around a reservoir and an old sewage works at Esholt, mid-way between the cities of Leeds and Bradford. Emmerdale, and its fictitious public house The Woolpack, even spawned a spin-off pop music group comprised of some of the cast. The eponymous Woolpackers had a top ten hit single in 1996, and an album that graced the lower reaches of the best-seller lists for almost three months, on the back of the craze for line-dancing that was rampant at that time.

Lancashire and Granada may have had their *Coronation Street*, but this could not compete with the natural scenery and the outside locations of Yorkshire. *All Creatures Great and Small*, based on the veterinary stories of James Herriot, was another hugely popular television programme set in the Yorkshire Dales. Latterly, there are programmes such as *Heartbeat* and *Dalziel and Pascoe*, which again benefit from the variety of spectacular and picturesque Yorkshire locations and countryside.

Other television series and programmes have used elements of the Yorkshire scenery, environment and ambience to great effect, for example, the use of Castle Howard as the setting for the series *Brideshead Revisited*, a classic British TV drama. The same can be said for numerous award-winning films for the cinema, such as *Calendar Girls*, *A Private Function* or *The Railway Children*, and even the more realistic and genuine urban and industrial settings used in movies such as *Kes*, *This Sporting Life*, *Room at the Top*, *Billy Liar*, and *The Full Monty*.

Interest in history at all levels – family, local, regional and national – and in archaeology and genealogy is stronger now than ever before. The phenomenal success of Friends Reunited, Genes Reunited and similar internet sites is irrefutable evidence of the growth of enthusiasm for the past and for nostalgia in general. It is also the direct result of new technologies putting the resources, techniques and skills of historical research within the compass of the wider population. History books and television series and documentaries appear regularly in the lists of bestsellers and the most viewed programmes.

The Yorkshire Dales figure largely in the best-selling series of crime mystery and suspense novels written by Peter Robinson, centred around the character of Detective Inspector Alan Banks (later promoted to Chief Inspector). The fictional setting of these excellent novels is the town of Eastvale, and places such as Swainsdale, Lyndgarth and Helmthorpe also feature. Not only are the stories first-class, but the mixture of fictional places within real locations and settings serves to add an extra element of interest in trying to identify the actual places and geography used. Some of the places to which Robinson refers may be fictional, but the descriptions and details of everyday lives, the personalities and lifestyles, the issues and concerns of the people of the Dales are given with precision and accuracy.

Historic Yorkshire is dedicated first and foremost to Johnny Wardle, and also to Geoff Boycott, Fred Trueman and the rest of the players and staff, past and present, of Yorkshire County Cricket Club, for the pleasure and elation, frustration and anguish that Yorkshire CCC has brought to spectators and fans over the years. There have been times in recent years when it has not been easy to be a follower of Yorkshire cricket, but loyalty to the White Rose is paramount. Geoff Boycott and Fred Trueman are instantly recognisable and are household names inside and outside of Yorkshire, but Johnny Wardle is probably less readily known or easily remembered.

Johnny Wardle is a particular hero of mine and one of the more forgotten men of Yorkshire and England cricket. Johnny Wardle's house was located in the road that ran immediately behind the house next door to my paternal grandfather and his daughter and family (that is my aunt, uncle and cousins) in Wakefield during the 1950s. Johnny was born at Ardsley, just a few miles away further along the road to Barnsley, in 1923. He was chosen as Wisden Cricketer of the Year in 1954, and South African Annual Cricketer of the Year in 1957.

As a left-hand batsman and slow left-arm bowler he had a formidable career as a first-class player for Yorkshire (1946–1958) and England (1947–1957) and played many times for the MCC and other representative sides. In his twenty-eight matches for England, the record shows that he took 102 wickets for 2,080 runs, from a total of 6,597 balls, including 403 maiden overs. (This was at a time when eight ball overs were played in some matches in Australia etc., so the conversion to wickets in terms of overs is not so easy to make). His best performance as an England bowler was seven for thirty-six; he took five wickets in an innings on five occasions; and once achieved the singular feat of ten wickets in an innings. As a batsman for England in forty-one innings (in the twenty-eight matches he played) he scored 653 runs, at an average of 19.78, with a highest score of sixty-six, and played two innings of fifty or more, and took twelve catches in the field. In terms of more modern cricketing statistics, with an average of one wicket in every twenty balls, and a batting average of almost twenty runs, this compares more than favourably with many of the so-called 'stars' of the current era. Overall, in his first-class career with Yorkshire, the MCC and England he made 7,333 runs and took 1,846 wickets, with his best performance being nine wickets for twenty-five runs, and a highest score of seventy-nine runs. He died in 1985 in Doncaster.

To my chagrin and regret, I personally do not remember much of the man who lived nearby my grandfather's and the family home. I was an infant or fairly young child at the time. Johnny was seemingly nearly always absent from home, either playing at home or away with the county, or on tour elsewhere in the country, or on overseas duty with the national team. I do, however, remember the silken tassels on the collection of county and national cricket caps and all the other cricketing memorabilia to be found in the house just behind my grandfather's. My elder brothers, who were of a similar age to Johnny's own son, remember Johnny and his son better than I do. They even played cricket together on many occasions either on the shale road that separated the houses or on the neighbouring green immediately opposite the houses across the main road.

I do vaguely remember an occasion when the fathers, uncles, sons and assorted neighbours from Bradford Road and St John's (including Johnny himself) all played in an impromptu local game or 'match' on that red shale road at the back of the houses. I can't recall the day in much detail and, on balance, I wonder if this really is a genuine memory or more of an 'acquired memory' garnered from the experience of my elder siblings. I do recall that, at that time, cricket was the game we played out in the streets and at the local recreation grounds and parks when we were young lads and in our early teens, and not soccer, rugby football, tennis or anything else.

My family always referred to and remembered Johnny Wardle as 'a real gentleman, generous, genuine and unassuming.' This amounts to as much of an accolade as a Yorkshireman is readily prepared to give or to receive. In my opinion, he was just the 'right stuff' for a schoolboy's hero. Moreover, he was left-handed and a ready role model for a left-handed boy at a time when left-handedness was often looked down on or even actively discouraged. Although naturally left-handed in all other things, I personally play cricket as if I were a natural right-handed player. I both bat right-handed and bowl right-handed. This does not mean that I am ambidextrous, but rather that I was taught how to play cricket by players and coaches who themselves were right-handed, and that was the natural way to hold the bat and ball as far as they were concerned.

My other heroes of Yorkshire cricket, apart from Wardle, Boycott and Trueman, must include Chris Old, Brian Close, Ray Illingworth, David Bairstow, Arnie Sidebottom, Darren Gough, Martyn Moxon, Phil Sharpe, Matthew Hoggard; the list goes on and on. Geoff Boycott in the early days of his career used to play cricket wearing his spectacles; another reason why a boy with glasses should look up to and respect such a stalwart of the Yorkshire county and England team. Boycott writes in his autobiography of his despair at being told as a boy that he would have to wear glasses and how he feared that this would be the end of a possible and promising cricketing career. With the help and support of M. J. K. Smith of Warwickshire, another leading player who also played in glasses, he solved the problem by wearing special rimless frames with shatterproof lenses.

This reminds me of the time when I was told that I would have to wear glasses. I had just started school and the teachers in the infant class were concerned about the general untidiness of my work, especially when trying to copy from the board. However, I remember I had just made a drawing of a sabre-tooth tiger, copied from a picture in one of my books, which was very detailed, neat and accurate. Control of the pencil and hand-eye coordination was obviously not the problem: maybe I could not see the blackboard properly. The teacher suggested that perhaps my sight needed checking.

I duly went with my mother to the local optician's on the following Saturday morning and the tests showed I would need glasses. I was totally and utterly devastated, not realising that there was any problem with my eyesight. How was I to know the world was not really always a bit fuzzy round the edges in the near distance, and not all that distinct when further away? Anyway, I was told not to worry – it would not be for long, for I would soon grow out of them and would not need glasses anymore. What absolute liars unthinking adults can be when talking to young children! That was more than five decades ago, and I am still waiting to 'grow out of them'. In the meantime the opticians' and optometrist industry has made a small fortune out of me for the many pairs of spectacles I have bought and worn since then.

My copy of the autobiography of Geoff Boycott, referred to above, was personally signed for me by Geoff at a book-signing in a local bookshop when I was living in South London. While he was writing the dedication I told him that we had met before, once near Hemsworth in the village where he used to live, and on another occasion at nearby Bretton Hall and its Sculpture Park. We then chatted about what he was doing for the media now that his playing career was over and about the future of cricket generally. When he asked me what a native-born Yorkshire lad, and one with my accent, was doing in Bromley, South London and I answered, 'Missionary work': he was, at first, not very amused. 'It's my job to tell the jokes if you don't mind!' was his initial retort. Then he smiled, burst out laughing, and said that I would have plenty of work cut out in trying to educate and convert these southerners and he wished me luck. I never got the chance to tell him my personal 'glasses' story, as the crowd behind in the shop waiting for their chance to get their copies signed was getting restless.

Who was it who said 'Nostalgia is not what it used to be'? Actually, it's better. I close this introduction with a few words written in the spirit of one of the most, if not the most, influential poets and spokesmen of my particular generation. In speaking about the universal truths of the arrogance of youth and the maturity and wisdom given by age and experience, I agree with him when he comments that: 'he used to feel so much older, wiser, better, and so certain then, but I am so much younger now.' There is no doubt that things have changed.

Finally, I think I need to add a note about political correctness and the deliberate use of the term Yorkshireman throughout this book. Yorkshireman is intended to be inclusive, and it is all-inclusive, and does not rule out the women of Yorkshire or Yorkshire children or anyone else. Yorkshire person or Yorkshire people, or any other supposedly PC alternative, does not have the same historical, social or political significance and is not instantly recognisable. The term Yorkshireman has served for centuries and will do perfectly well for me and, I trust, for my readers. As for the use of the term 'tyke', that is not a term of abuse in Yorkshire but has a specific meaning within the county. A 'loveable rogue' is the nearest general equivalent, I suppose, for the rest of the country. As far as I am concerned, the characters of Compo or perhaps Cleggie in the BBC's *Last of the Summer Wine* are the epitome of a typical Yorkshire tyke. Perhaps that explains much of the appeal of the programme. Yorkshire men and women have a good sense of humour. They especially like jokes and stories told about themselves, but only when told by another Yorkshireman. Anything else is just, as Norah Batty would say in the more recent series of *Last of the Summer Wine*, 'I can't be doing with that . . .' And quite right, too! I concur whole-heartedly.

Many years ago, I overheard a phrase that has since become a regular saying or 'catchphrase' among the family and within our circle of friends. (My all-time favourite example of the 'eavesdrop' is the two elderly ladies overheard on a London bus discussing the issues of marriage, death and surviving partners. One of the ladies added, 'My husband and I have discussed this, and we've agreed that whichever one of us goes first, then I'll go and live with my sister in Bournemouth.')

It was mid-morning in late summer or early autumn, depending on how optimistic you felt about the weather, and the day looked as if it could well begin to rain before too long. We were crossing the car park at Ilkley railway station, when a group of ramblers passed by going in the opposite direction. The last couple in the group were stragglers at the rear. They were a man and a woman, probably in their early forties and, judging by the accent, probably from Bolton, but certainly from the North Manchester area. As they passed by us we heard with absolute clarity the man make an almost plaintive response (not quite despairing but in no way reassuring either) to something his partner had just said: 'Oh, No, Cynthia! It'll not come to that!' Almost as soon as we overheard this, the party was gone heading off for the day's outing at a rapid pace, while we went the other way looking for the next train with only a few minutes to spare.

Whatever it was that Cynthia was so worried and anxious about, I do not know, but I have often speculated about what the 'it' could have been. However, after living for some considerable time now in Spain, specifically in Barcelona, I am now thoroughly convinced of one thing. It most certainly did come to 'that', whatever the 'that' was which Cynthia and her male companion were so concerned about. Why do I think this? Whatever trouble or concern there was in Cynthia's life at that particular time, human nature being what it is means that, more often than not, what we fear or want to avoid will inevitably happen. Life does strange and bizarre things from time to time. Either that or it is just plain daft sometimes. This story has also served as a sort of everyday reminder of the unpredictable and sometimes quixotic nature of life and experience.

Richard A. Powell, Barcelona, 2009

(The cover design for the original volumes was by Roger Hitchen, as are some of the drawings in the text. Other illustrations are taken from old prints. Photographs for the new revised edition are by Phil Burchell and Sam Powell.)

Chapter One

Prehistoric Yorkshire

In 10,000 BC, the last ice sheet covering northern Britain finally melted and the Ice Age came to an end. We know only a little about the men who lived at that time, but it is possible to formulate some impressions about their way of life. These people were hunters and they lived and sheltered in caves, which were especially prevalent in limestone areas. In one early settlement, Victoria Cave, near Settle, remains have been found which date back to the Upper Palaeolithic period. Although these early men have left behind them only a few bone and flint implements, they were able to make fire and they knew how to chip flint and make sharp cutting edges. Their way of life was nomadic as they followed the herds of wild animals that they hunted for food.

Thousands of years later this way of life had altered little, although men were capable of making much better tools, weapons and implements, such as antler harpoons and arrowheads, and bone fish-hooks. Remains found at Star Carr, near Seamer, are dated about 7,500 BC, and show that man still lived almost entirely by hunting animals such as bear, boar, deer, wild sheep and cattle. Other finds from this age have been found in Yorkshire in the caves around Malham, and on the shoreline at Hornsea and Skipsea. However, advanced as these finds are from the simple flint scrapers found at Settle, they are still the products of a hunting people with no apparent knowledge of agriculture.

Farming was introduced by the peoples of the New Stone Age, or Neolithic period, in about 2,500 BC. It seems likely that these people originally came from the Mediterranean lands and, as they were primarily agriculturalists, they were the first men to make fairly permanent settlements and build houses. These people were different from their predecessors, not only in clearing and cultivating land and living in established dwellings, but also making simple pottery and clothes. These New Stone Age peoples still preferred to live in upland areas as the valleys were mainly masses of undergrowth and swamp, and dense forests covered much of the rest of the countryside. Chalk and limestone areas, with their poor soils and thin vegetative cover, were obvious choices for the early men to make settlements. Coastal locations were also popular sites for these peoples to make settlements.

Neolithic man appears to have had some simple religious beliefs. They buried their dead in long or circular mounds known as barrows. Other earthworks, tumuli, monuments and stone circles testify to the relatively advanced state of civilisation that these people reached.

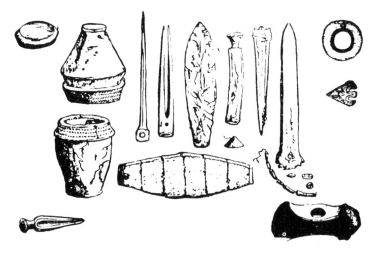

The custom of burying weapons, food and pottery with the dead has supplied many of the artefacts found from this period. This practice suggests that Neolithic man had some notion of a life after death since care was taken to ensure that corpses were interred with items of early wealth and importance.

At Ulrome, near Bridlington, some more unusual dwellings have been discovered. This settlement was built along the shores of a lake and, to afford extra protection, the houses were constructed on wooden piles above the water level. Completely made of wood, the living platform forming the floor of the dwelling was later covered by additional levels and floors. It is from these different levels that many important discoveries have been made. Bones of domestic and wild animals were found, including those of wolves, boars, horses, pigs, dogs and sheep. Flint tools and weapons, stone hammers, pieces and fragments of earthenware pottery and round grinding stones for crushing corn have also been discovered.

About 2,000 BC the next wave of immigrants became established in Yorkshire. Generally known as the Beaker people because of their skill in making beaker-shaped pots, these men also knew how to make bronze. There are Bronze Age settlements and remains at Ilkley, Brough, Great Ayton and Eston, as well as monuments, such as the Devil's Arrows, near Boroughbridge. The Yorkshire Wolds are particularly rich in Bronze Age barrows and burial chambers, pottery, weapons, ornaments and other artefacts. It is probable that these people traded with the Continent and Ireland. One trade route from Scandinavia to Ireland is believed to have crossed Ilkley and Rombalds Moor, where many Bronze Age remains have been discovered.

In time, the Bronze Age people were conquered by a new wave of invaders who had mastered the art of making iron tools and weapons. This new Iron Age soon replaced bronze since the new metal of iron combined toughness and pliability, as well as enabling the working of sharp edges and points; qualities which were lacking in bronze.

One particular group of Iron Age men arrived in about 300 BC from Gaul and they belonged to a race known as the Celts. The Celtic people were a warlike race who combined their military sense with an ability to make strong, sharp, iron weapons and chariots with iron wheels. Two burial sites have been discovered in Yorkshire, at Pickering and Dane's Graves, near Driffield, where whole chariots were buried. These chariots are constructed with wheels with iron rims and tyres, iron pins and rings, and with many items and elements of the driving tackle also made from iron and bronze. It is the descendants of these Celts who, as the first true Britons, resisted the Roman invaders with great ferocity.

One of their major hilltop settlements was on the summit of Ingleborough (2,376ft) and it is likely that this fort of the Brigantes was constructed to oppose the otherwise all-conquering Romans. Although the Celtic tribes bitterly resented and opposed the Romans, they proved to be unsuccessful due to factions, tribal rivalries, and fighting amongst themselves. As Tacitus, the Roman historian, wrote: 'It is seldom that even two or three of these tribes will join in meeting a common enemy: so while each fights for himself, they are all conquered together.'

The written history of Yorkshire begins with the Romans, who by the year AD 70 were firmly established in Northern England in spite of attacks from the Brigantes. Of the importance of the Roman occupation in Yorkshire, and the surviving traces of it, one writer says:

> In the abundance and variety of its Roman antiquities, Yorkshire stands second to no other county. We find camps, signal stations, fortresses, houses, villages, towns; iron-mines, lead-mines, potteries; baths, amphitheatres, temples; cemeteries, inscriptions, altars; and a thousand and one objects of daily life, from the shells gathered by children at the seaside to the jet pins which still adorn the dark hair of one whose beauty otherwise is dust.

Of the remains of pre-Roman Yorkshire, the many place-names of Ancient British origin should be particularly noted. The British kingdom of Elmet, which stretched from the Pennines to the Humber, still survives today in the village names of Barwick-in-Elmet and Sherburn-in-Elmet. Many of Yorkshire's rivers have British names, such as the Derwent, Tees, Esk, Ure, Calder, Don, Aire and Wharfe. Most of Yorkshire's towns and villages, however, have Anglo-Saxon or Danish (Viking) names. Leeds is an exception to this, its name being derived from Loidis, a British name. But the main relics of prehistoric Yorkshire consist of the many earthworks, burial mounds, cave settlements, to be found on the hillsides, hilltops and on the moors, as well as the ancient trackways, which mark the beginnings of Yorkshire's road system.

Left: *A celt and his coracle.*

Below: *Old Roman coins.*

Chapter Two

Roman Yorkshire

Yorkshire contains a large number and variety of relics and remains of the Roman occupation. Prominent among these are the remains of forts, marching camps, villas, signal stations, a road network, towns, and a legionary fortress and colonia. It is somewhat of an anachronism, however, to talk of Roman Yorkshire since 'the county, or shire, is of Anglo-Saxon or Danish origin, and does not correspond to any civil or military unit known to Roman Britain.' With this cautionary note in mind, it is not too surprising that Yorkshire still bears traces of Roman times for they ruled Yorkshire for almost 350 years.

Although the Romans first invaded England in 55 BC, and returned the following year for another short stay, it was not until almost a century later that the conquest of Britain began in earnest. In AD 43 the Emperor Claudius (AD 41–54) led an expedition to Britain which quickly overran most of Southern England and established a permanent base for the occupation. The invasion had been prevented from moving northwards and westwards by fierce warlike tribes who resisted the early attempts of the Roman legions to subdue them. At that time Yorkshire was inhabited by two such tribes: the Brigantes who lived in the Pennines and the west, and the Parisi who belonged to East Yorkshire and the Wolds. Outbreaks of civil war in Brigantia in AD 51 and AD 69 upset the tentative alliance to which the Romans and Brigantes had agreed in AD 43. On both occasions the Roman forces had intervened on behalf of the Brigantian rulers. The Romans, under their general Petillius Cerialis, were then ordered by the Emperor Vespasian (AD 69–79) to invade and conquer Brigantia and settle the troubles once and for all.

Thus in AD 71, Cerialis came north with the IX Legion from their headquarters at Lincoln and advanced to York, where he founded a legionary fortress at a previous Brigantian settlement known as Eburach, situated on an island at the junction of the rivers Ouse and Foss. The Brigantes were quickly and ruthlessly crushed. The Roman forces started to construct a more permanent base from which they could organise further expeditions to meet resistance from the remaining tribes. In AD 74 Cerialis was recalled to Rome and was succeeded as governor of Britain by Julius Frontinus. Frontinus was fully occupied by conflict with the Silures in Wales and made no attempt to extend the northern frontiers. He was replaced in AD 77 by Julius Agricola who, during his period of governership until his recall in AD 85 by the Emperor Domitian, became the greatest of all Roman governors. It was Agricola who undertook the

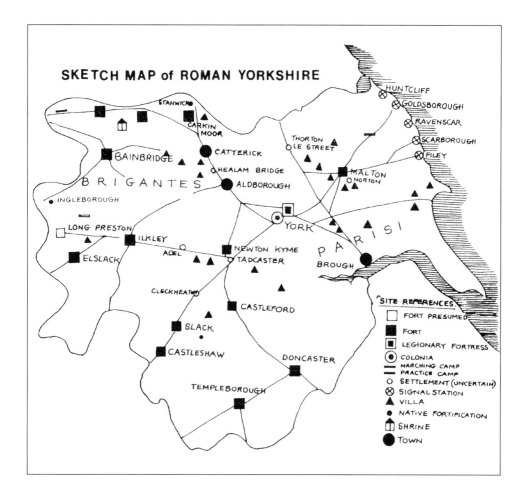

SKETCH MAP of ROMAN YORKSHIRE

SITE REFERENCES

- ☐ FORT PRESUMED
- ■ FORT
- ▣ LEGIONARY FORTRESS
- ◉ COLONIA
- ▬ MARCHING CAMP
- ▬ PRACTICE CAMP
- ○ SETTLEMENT (UNCERTAIN)
- ⊗ SIGNAL STATION
- ▲ VILLA
- • NATIVE FORTIFICATION
- ⌂ SHRINE
- ● TOWN

systematic subordination of Brigantia to Roman rule. Agricola launched a series of campaigns and offensives against the pockets of native resistance to the occupation. Under Agricola much of Wales was pacified, the Brigantes were quietened, and the Romans pushed north reaching as far as the rivers Forth and Clyde in Scotland. For these operations in the north, Eboracum (York) – as the Romans renamed the former Brigantian settlement of Eburach – was the natural choice as a base for the troops. The defences at Eboracum were reinforced through the building of trenches and earth ramparts. The fortress at Eboracum quickly became established as a centre of great military importance.

During the rule of Agricola, the first permanent forts and a connecting road system were built in Yorkshire. Several auxiliary forts were built to ensure effective control of the county. The forts guarding the Pennines were at Bowes (Lavatrae), Bainbridge (Virosidum), Greta Bridge (Maglona), Elslack, Ilkley (Olicana), Slack (Camulodonum), Cattleshaw and Templeborough. Forts in East Yorkshire were established at Brough (Petuaria), Malton (Derventio) and Aldborough (Isurium Brigantium). These early forts were built of timber with earthen ramparts and surrounded by wooden palisades with towers and gates. Later they were greatly strengthened by the replacement of timber with stone.

5

Far more important than these early forts were the roads that connected them. Indeed it has been said that, 'the great legacy of the Romans to the Yorkshire of today is the Roman road system.' Traces of these roads remain in almost every part of Yorkshire, and the routes of many are still in use today. These roads were built with the express purpose of serving the military camps and forts, providing an easy and rapid means of access for reinforcements should any of these forts come under attack. Usually they followed the natural lines of communication afforded by the geography of the area but, wherever possible, they took a straight and undeviating course. This is especially true of the major roads that run the length and breadth of the county in long, straight stretches for mile after mile.

The major route through the county of Yorkshire formed part of Ermine Street and ran from Piercebridge on the Tees in the north to Doncaster in the south. The forts of Aldborough and Catterick (Cataractonium) were sited on the road itself. This road was crossed by an east-west track connecting York to Ermine Street and extending westwards into the Pennines. East Yorkshire was served by a road network based on Brough, Malton and York. Tadcaster (Calcaria) marked another crossing-point of the north-south and east-west roads. The forts at Elslack and Ilkley guarded the roads that crossed the Pennines through the Aire gap.

Once the road system became established, the Romans then began to take stock of the natural resources of the county. Lead mines were opened in Wharfedale, Nidderdale and Swaledale. Agriculture was encouraged by the felling of forests and the draining of swamps, while the provision of roads gave the opportunity of transporting produce to the rapidly developing Roman towns. Quarrying was established at Tadcaster, and possibly at Castleford (Lagentium), in order to provide the stone to build stronger defences. During the reign of Emperor Trajan (AD 98–117) many forts were rebuilt with stone. Eboracum was rebuilt in AD 107–108 with stone walls. Gates and towers were placed at intervals along the walls and at the angles between them. The tower built to protect the south-west corner of the camp still remains and is known as the Multangular Tower because of its ten sides. Among the other industries introduced by the Romans were pottery and brick-making. A pottery was established at Malton to provide all the pots required by the army.

Hadrian, who became Emperor in AD 117, came to visit Britain in AD 122. It was Hadrian who ordered the construction of a fortified wall between the Tyne and Solway Firth to keep the barbarians of the far north, the Picts and the Scots, at bay. The completion of Hadrian's Wall in AD 138 marked the end of any serious Brigantian threat to the Roman power. Moreover, the wall consolidated the position of Eboracum as the foremost northern outpost, since the fortress at Eboracum was responsible for this furthest branch of the Empire. Hadrian also replaced the garrison at Eboracum with the VI Legion when the IX Legion was posted overseas. The VI Legion was to remain stationed at Eboracum for almost 300 years, until the end of the fourth century, when the complete Roman withdrawal was ordered.

Hadrian was succeeded as Emperor by Antoninus Pius (AD 138–161) who built the Antonine Wall between the Forth and the Clyde after a campaign of re-occupation in Scotland. The completion of this wall led to considerable unrest in Brigantia, Northern England and Scotland, while the pushing of the Empire's frontier further to the north meant greater strains on the troops left behind to garrison the area. There were several outbreaks of revolt and attacks on forts, which brought a second reoccupation of the Pennines in AD 150–160. Forty years or so later, in AD 196, some of the troops in Northern England were withdrawn to help with the fighting in Gaul. The tribes in the north broke through Hadrian's Wall and Brigantia once more was stirred to revolt, resulting in the destruction of many Roman forts in Yorkshire.

The Emperor Septimius Severus (AD 193–211) himself came to Britain to restore Roman rule. He first arrived in Eboracum in AD 208 on his way to Scotland to quell the rebellion and rebuild the wall and returned there in AD 211 where he died on 4 February at the age of seventy-three. Eboracum, by this time, had swollen in size and now included a prosperous chartered town, or colonia, and had become the capital of the province of Lower Britain, or Britannia Inferior as the Romans knew it.

After the troubles with the Caledonians had ended, the next few decades were a time of fairly peaceful co-existence between the Roman invaders and the native Britons. The prosperity of the Roman rule and the lasting peace were beneficial to most people, whether it was through increased trade, better communications or the developing industries that the Romans helped to foster. At this time, many Roman villas and palaces were built to house the Roman noblemen and aristocracy, while the native peasants were often attracted to the small towns and villages that sprang up near the Roman camps and stations. Many of the young Britons served in the Roman armies for a time. They were paid wages which helped to attract merchants and traders to the military camps. Together with the soldiers' families and other camp followers, the Roman garrison towns grew to quite large proportions. Usually, the British recruits in the Legions were sent to do guard duty on the wall and in the borderlands, so that the experienced Roman soldiers were kept behind in reserve should they be required. The relative calm of the third century produced little unrest and there was little need to call on the military and use force of arms.

One of Yorkshire's most striking Roman remains is the military road of Wheeldale Moor, near Goathland. It ran from Malton by way of Cawthorn Camp towards Eskdale. (S. Outram)

This peace and calm was interrupted in the closing years of the century when Allectus seized the governership of Britain by murdering the previous holder of the office. This action brought about an invasion from Rome led by Constantius in AD 296. Constantius (AD 293–306) defeated Allectus and he also put down the northern tribes who had used the Roman disturbances as an opportunity to cross the wall and raid and burn the Yorkshire forts. Constantius then rebuilt the camps and also made additions to the defences at Eboracum. He also divided Britain into four provinces and made Eboracum the capital of a new military governor called the Dux Britanniarum. When Constantius died at Eboracum in AD 306, his son Constantine (AD 306–337) was proclaimed as Emperor in July of that same year. Eboracum was now at the height of its glory and was a magnificent city, truly fitting for a new Emperor. Constantine's reign was the start of another period of calm during which the Romanisation of Britain spread further and further outwards among the Britons.

However, once more these peaceful times were to be disturbed. This time it was a series of raids by Saxons, Angles, Picts and Scots during AD 367–369, which again caused much damage. The invasion forces of the Angles and Saxons had come by sea and landed at various points on the coast. It was against this threat that the Romans decided to build up a new series of coastal defences. At several points on the Yorkshire coast – Huntcliff, Goldsborough, Ravenscar, Scarborough and Filey, in order from north to south – a number of signal stations were erected which would provide an early warning system for impending invasions. These signal stations were tall strong towers built on prominences near the coast and where beacon fires could be lighted if any threatened attack was spotted. Reinforcements could be quickly dispatched to the coast from the forts at York or Malton once the warning was given. These measures proved highly successful in maintaining security.

By AD 400 this situation had drastically altered. Roman troops had been withdrawn from Britain to protect the city of Rome itself from invaders. The British signal stations had been captured and burnt by Saxons, who quickly took advantage of reductions in the Roman strength. Further withdrawals of troops in AD 407–411 marked the final end of the Roman occupation. In AD 410 the Emperor Honorius (AD 395–423, Emperor of the Western Empire) advised the British peoples and the British towns to organise their own defences against the invaders.

And so after 350 years the Romans left Yorkshire, to which they had given so much and which had prospered so greatly during their presence. They were to be replaced by successions of invaders – first the Angles and the Saxons, then the Vikings and later the Normans. These later waves of peoples were to leave many traces of their influence and cultures. Inevitably, these new invasions wiped out much of the Roman remains and their distinctive monuments. However, the Roman legacy and heritage has not disappeared altogether and many relics and remnants are still left to remind us of those glorious days of Empire when Yorkshire boasted many thriving Roman communities, and the major city of Eboracum, which in its golden age was rightly called the 'Altera Roma'.

The centuries of Roman rule had given much to Britain but it had not left the Britons able to defend themselves. When the Roman legions left, as one writer has said: 'It was not Britain that broke loose from the Empire but the Empire that gave up Britain.' The troubled times that followed the Roman withdrawal reduced the name of Rome to no more than a splendid memory, and it is the memory of those days of Empire that the county of Yorkshire is so fortunate in calling to mind with its wealth and variety of Roman relics and remains.

Chapter Three

Yorkshire Castles

The castles of Yorkshire are remarkable for their number and strength and, in the days past, were also of no mean importance. The many stories around these castles are woven into the closest strands of national history. Originally built to keep the Northumbrians in check and the warlike Northland at bay, rather than to protect the Borders, the fortresses of Yorkshire offer fine examples of every type of medieval stronghold. In keeping with medieval military fashion, these fortresses were so positioned as to take every advantage that the natural site and geography could offer. These castles were built on rocky crags, on storm-ravaged cliffs, by the side of rivers or along the coasts. In keeping with the accepted stubborn or obdurate trait in the Yorkshire county character, Yorkshire castles obstinately refused to yield even in the face of the most alarming odds.

Strongholds such as Pontefract, York, Knaresborough, Richmond, Skipton and Scarborough have achieved lasting fame for past deeds and incidents, but Yorkshire also boasts a number of lesser known fortresses such as Barwick-in-Elmet, Malton, Mexborough, Middleham, Ravensworth and Topcliffe. Besides these, the county also has many fine examples of fortified houses which, for the most part, have been recorded as castles in historical records and documents.

The difference between a fortified house and a castle lies in the emphasis placed on defence. The castle proper was, first and foremost, a military stronghold. The fortified house was, above all else, a home. Harewood, Spofforth and Wressle Castles spring to mind as examples of the fortified house. Medieval houses, apart from offering shelter and comfort, were also designed to withstand the onslaught of a raiding party and to resist attacks not only from across the Borders but also from marauding outlaws engaged in robbery.

For the most part, all that remains of these former strongholds amounts to nothing more than a few ruins. Isolated examples are, however, far more fortunate, with enough of the former structure remaining to give at least some indication of past significance. The remnants and vestiges of these fortresses stand out against the country skyline as a constant reminder of those troubled times which produced not only these magnificent edifices but also the need for them. Less fortunate are those castles now in total ruins and completely destroyed. They are only able to give us a glimpse into that distant and remote backcloth of history, which is an essential and integral part of our cultural heritage.

Pontefract Castle owes its origins to William the Conqueror. In 1069, while *en route* for York to put down a rebellion of English and Danish rivals, William was halted at the banks of the River Aire. The Danes, who had appeared in the Humber estuary with a great fleet of ships, had combined forces with those English nobles who had fled before the Norman invaders after the Battle of Hastings. But the Aire was in flood and so kept the Norman army delayed and in check for three weeks. During that enforced stay or sojourn, William discovered an ideal natural site, overlooking the River Aire and commanding the surrounding plains, to build a fortress which would become known as the 'Key of the North'. When the floodwaters of the Aire subsided, William was able to continue on his march to meet this challenge from the Danes and the rebel nobles in the north. By the time he reached York, the Danes had fled, and the English nobles had retreated over the borders into Scotland to avoid the avenging Normans. William was not to be so easily averted and, determined to stop these insurrections for good, he put the whole of the northern countryside to the sword: killing many of the peasants – men, women and children; burning down farmsteads and destroyed cattle and other livestock; and setting fire to the crops. The north of England was left as a scorched wilderness completely desolated by the angry King.

Returning from York, William gave to Ilbert de Lacy, one of his captains, a vast stretch of land extending from the River Trent to the far west. Together with this gift of land, William also gave de Lacy instructions to watch over these troubled lands for his sovereign. It was de Lacy who built the castle on the site later to become known as Pontefract. The castle of Ilbert, as it was described in the Domesday Book, remained in the ownership of the de Lacy family for over 200 years. Henry de Lacy not only inherited the estates, but he also founded the Cistercian Abbey of Kirkstall.

When the de Lacy line became extinct with the death of Henry de Lacy, Earl of Lincoln, the estates passed to Henry's son-in-law, Thomas of Lancaster. Thomas turned rebel against King Edward II. In 1322, Thomas was captured by King Edward's men after the Battle of Boroughbridge. For his rebellion he was executed without trial since, being caught red-handed in open revolt, he had no defence to offer. Being of royal blood, the Earl escaped the usual severity of the penalty for traitors and was spared being hanged, drawn and quartered, before facing the headman's axe.

Edward III, who became King in 1327 after Edward II's reign had been foreshortened by the barons as a result of years of dissatisfaction, gave back the lands and castle of Pontefract to the Lancasters. Lancaster and York were much later to be united in the name of Tudor when Henry VII, a direct descendant of John of Gaunt, married Elizabeth of York, daughter of Edward IV.

The other name for Pontefract Castle, Pomfret, has been immortalised by Shakespeare, who portrays in the play *Richard II* the murder of the unfortunate King in the dungeon there. In the play it is Sir Piers Exton who wields the final sword-blow responsible for that pitiful regicide. But the Exton legend only gained credence nearly 100 years after the mysterious death. Richard II most certainly died at Pontefract Castle, but it is probably nearer the truth to say that he suffered death from starvation rather than to maintain that he was foully and cruelly slain by the unwilling Bolingbroke's henchmen.

Pontefract re-emerges at the forefront of national events during the Civil War when the Parliamentarians rose against Charles I, forcing the King to set up his standard at Nottingham on 22 August 1642, as a preliminary to the years of bloody warfare and tragedy that were

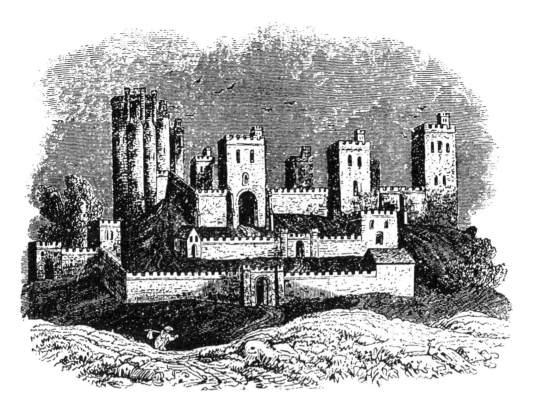

Pontefract Castle, which played such a prominent part in the story of medieval Yorkshire. Today little of the building remains.

to follow. All the Yorkshire castles and fortresses remained loyal to the King, bar the city of Hull, which held out against Newcastle and the King's cavaliers, and supported Fairfax and the Parliamentarians.

Fairfax laid siege to York in 1644 but Prince Rupert, by a brilliant manoeuvre, relieved the city. Rupert, not content to let his enemies disperse, offered battle although the Royalists were outnumbered three to one. The resulting conflict took place at Marston Moor on 2 July 1644. The day went badly for the King with the hitherto invincible Rupert defeated at last. The cavaliers fought well, being likened by their enemies to an iron wall. Their defeat was a notable achievement. Prince Rupert, who was regarded by many as commanding the best troops in Europe, said of his army: 'I am sure they fought well, and therefore know of no reason for my rout but this, because the devil did help his servants.' The fugitive Royalists from the battle escaped to Pontefract Castle in order to join the already strong garrison there which was under the command of Sir Richard Lowther.

Fairfax arrived at Pontefract in December 1644, well prepared to lay siege to this important Royalist stronghold. The Piper Tower of the castle fell on 19 January 1645 after three days of heavy bombardment. Fairfax was not able to make any further breach in the castle walls. This caused little inconvenience to the garrison who had previously taken the precaution of filling in the postern door and the hollow of the tower before its eventual fall. Fairfax next tried the tactic of undermining the walls of the castle – and again achieved little success. Colonel Lambert then assumed command as Fairfax was recalled. A Royalist relief force attacked Lambert on 1 March 1645. They raised the siege, and managed to re-provision and reinforce the garrison.

The second attempt on the castle commenced on 21 March 1645 when a stronger force of Parliamentarians, under Colonel Forbes, entered the town. The Roundhead force seized the heights of nearby Monkhill and Baghill and began to install artillery for a second and more intense bombardment. On 12 June, Colonel Poyntz superseded Forbes and began a more sustained assault on the castle. 14 June 1645 was a memorable day for Cromwell and the Parliamentarians with the decisive victory at the Battle of Naseby. This proved to be the beginning of the total ruin of the Royalist cause. News of this defeat at Naseby reached Pontefract. The Royalists immediately realised that there could be little hope of relief or any provisions getting through the besieging forces, who were rapidly increasing in strength and numbers. Food and ammunition within the castle ran low and eventually and inevitably petered out. Lowther had no alternative but to arrange a surrender and, on 28 July, he handed the castle over to the Parliamentarians. In the four months of the siege, the Parliamentarian force had lost 469 men; the Royalists had only ninety-nine fatalities.

The Parliamentarians considered the acquisition of the castle so important that they ordered after its surrender, that the fortress be maintained and garrisoned. Skipton and Scarborough castles were treated in like manner after they too had yielded to the forces of Parliament. The castle at Pontefract was to remain under Parliamentarian command until 1648. During that year, the Royalists managed to win back all three fortresses; being encouraged to do so by the proposed Royalist invasion from Scotland under the command of Hamilton. On 3 June, Colonel Morris, with a small band of followers, obtained entry to Pontefract, 'probably by treachery', and overcame the Parliamentarian garrison. Morris gathered in another 500 men and supplies, and prepared for another Parliamentarian siege, which was to be the longest yet.

Cromwell himself was present for a while at the third siege of Pontefract and he reported to the Parliamentarian headquarters about the castle as follows:

> The place is very well known to be one of the strongest inland garrisons of the kingdom, well watered, situate on a rock in every part of it and, therefore, difficult to mine. The walls are very thick and high, with strong towers and, if battered, very difficult of access by reason of the depth and steepness of the graft (ditch).

As a result of this report Parliament hurried supplies of powder, cannons, bullets and ball, shot, and heavy calibre mortars to be used to reduce this Royalist threat. Even so, the siege dragged on.

King Charles I was executed at Whitehall on 30 January 1649 and, on receiving the news, the garrison at Pontefract made a murderous sally in which no quarter was given. Colonel Morris, confident in the strength of his defensive position, proclaimed Charles II as King, and adopted the motto *post mortem patris pro filio* – after the death of the father we are for the son – and struck the first coins of the new reign.

Defeat was inevitable, however, no matter how heroic, tenacious and stubborn the Royalist defence. Hamilton had been soundly defeated at Preston, and the Royalist cause, all but for this isolated handful of men in Pontefract Castle, completely destroyed. When the food and powder ran out and after suffering severe losses during heavy bombardments, Colonel Morris had no option but to consider terms on which to yield up the castle. So on 24 March 1649, after many months of siege, the Royalist garrison marched out and laid down their weapons. The terms of surrender offered clemency to all save Colonel Morris and five others. These six were able to attempt escape, aided by the troops of the garrison, but one of them, Ensign Smith, was killed in the attempt. Colonel Morris and Cornet Blackburn escaped to Lancashire but were captured in April and taken to York. There, on 23 August after being quickly found guilty by jury, Morris was hanged, drawn and quartered for his part in the affair. The other three leaders were also refused clemency, and were declared to have been killed in the siege – but they were, in fact, ingeniously walled up in the postern of Piper Tower, from where they later escaped.

The castle itself was not to escape so lightly at the hands of Cromwell. Parliament ordered on 27 March 1649, that 'the Castle of Pontefract be forewith totally demolished.' Thus the fate of the many-towered Pontefract was sealed, and the fortress that had stood for nearly 600 years was carefully and thoroughly taken apart. It was determined that this magnificent fortress should never again offer shelter for belligerents or be occupied. The months of weary toil, siege, bombardment and storm had shortened Parliamentarian tempers against the Yorkshire fortresses that had held out against them for so long. The castles of Knaresborough, Sheffield, Cawood, Middleham, Bolton, Craike, Helmsley, Skipton and Wressle were to suffer the same ignominious end. And so, in a single stroke, Yorkshire was denuded of much of its former strength; its fortresses were desolated, leaving behind only the mere ruins of a previous, glorious past.

Sandal Castle, situated near Wakefield, has little to show of its once bold magnificence. However, the ruins that are left have been subject to a series of excavations by a team of archaeologists, who have uncovered much of the former foundations and subsequently found many articles of interest. The castle was built in the twelfth century, by the de Warrenne family, and was a wooden motte-and-bailey construction. Stone defences were added some time

Sandal Castle, near Wakefield, destroyed in 1648. The remains have recently been excavated.

later, probably by John, the seventh Earl de Warrenne (1240–1304). He was succeeded by his grandson, the 8th and last Earl, who was also named John. This Earl John became involved in a feud with Thomas of Lancaster, who came from nearby Pontefract, and whose wife Earl John had apparently carried off by force in 1317 to his castle at Reigate in Sussex.

In revenge for this deed, Thomas of Lancaster took Sandal Castle and burned it to the ground. He then seized Conisbrough Castle, which also belonged to John de Warrenne. Thomas was allowed to retain Sandal and the manor of Wakefield on final settlement of the dispute but, as we have already seen, this success was to be short-lived. At Lancaster's trial, in his own castle at Pontefract, one of his judges was John de Warrenne. After Lancaster's execution, the castle was restored to de Warrenne in 1328, who then began its reconstruction. John de Warrenne, the 8th Earl, had no legitimate heir. On the death of his widow, his lands reverted to the Crown. Edward II made a gift of the estate to his son Edmund de Langley, who later left it in turn to his son, Edward. Edward was killed at Agincourt in 1415. His nephew Richard, Duke of York, was to inherit next.

In 1460, Richard of York declared himself King and, with his Yorkist supporters, made camp at Sandal. The Lancastrians, based at Pontefract, were believed to number between 15,000 and 20,000 men. Richard of York was said 'to have but a fifth of this number'. On 30 December 1460, a Yorkist foraging party was set upon by a small Lancastrian force. Richard left his fortress together with all his troops in an attempt to rescue the foragers. However, the main Lancastrian army was waiting in ambush for the Yorkists. As they reached the bridge over the River Calder, the Yorkists found that their retreat had been cut off. Hemmed in on every side, the Battle of Wakefield Bridge proved to be a massacre and, in the ensuing conflict, Richard of York was killed.

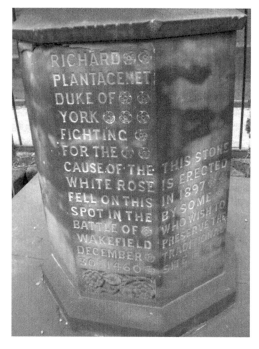

Battle of Wakefield monument.

It was during this battle at Wakefield that Clifford, Earl of Lancaster, gained the reputation and nickname of the 'Butcher'. The reason for this is usually explained by the following incident: the Earl of Rutland, the Duke of York's twelve-year-old son, was leaving the battlefield when Clifford saw him and took him captive. At first Clifford did not recognise the boy. However, once he ascertained the true identity of his captive, he exclaimed: 'By God's Blood, thy father slew my father, and so will I do thee, and all thy kin!' With these words he drew his dagger and struck the young Earl to the heart. (Clifford was himself to die on the field of battle at Towton Field a few months later.)

The victorious Lancastrians, finding York and his son among the dead on the battlefield, cut off their heads and later left them impaled and exposed at Micklegate Bar in York, 'so that York may overlook the Town of York'. The city of York still retains the early names of the parts of the medieval walled city, which have been the source of some confusion in the past. The streets are generally termed as 'gates', the gatehouses are called 'bars', and the city walls are 'bar walls'. There were four principal gateways, or bars, which are still functioning today as entrances to the centre of the city. The entrance to the city from the south was through Micklegate Bar, which originally had a barbican that unfortunately now no longer exists. Micklegate Bar was built during the reign of Edward III and incorporates a much earlier Norman arch in its structure.

Micklegate Bar was traditionally used as a place to expose the heads of traitors. The head of Henry Percy was so exposed after his death in the battle of Shrewsbury in 1403, when he attempted to rebel against Henry IV. The Duke of York received a similar treatment in 1460 but his head was covered with a paper crown by his enemies as a final insult. His son, Edward, gained revenge for this in the following year after the Battle of Towton Field (where Clifford was to meet his end). Edward had journeyed to York as soon as the battle was won. There he was confronted with the ghastly sight of his father's head, horribly exposed, as he reached the city walls. Incensed by this, he ordered the immediate execution of his prisoners, the Earls of Devon and Wiltshire, and replaced his father's head with theirs. The last occasion that Micklegate Bar was used for the exhibition of traitors' heads was during the aftermath of the Jacobite Rebellion of 1745.

Other bars in York include Bootham Bar, which protected the entrance to the city from the north. Owing to almost continual disputes between England and Scotland, the gateway was always strongly guarded. At one time, all Scots who wished to enter the city were obliged to announce their arrival by using the rapper on the gate and were then expected to seek permission from the warder. Any Scot discovered in the city without the necessary permit of the lord mayor or a warder was liable to arrest and imprisonment. In much earlier times, armed guides could be obtained at Bootham Bar to protect those travelling north through the Forest of Galtres, where wolves were a serious hazard to be considered.

Monk Bar, which stands at the entrance to the city from Scarborough, was also built in the reign of Edward III. Originally called Goodramgate, it was renamed in honour of General Monk after the restoration of the monarchy in 1660. Walmgate Bar guards the entrance to the city from Hull. The Bar suffered heavily during the Parliamentarian artillery bombardment of 1644. The barbican, however, was repaired in 1648, and is the only gatehouse remaining of any of the Bars.

Sandal Castle, meanwhile, being left without a garrison, was easily overrun by a small Lancastrian detachment. The castle and estates then passed into the hands of Edward, Earl of

March, who later became Edward IV. The castle remained in the hands of the Crown until 1566 when Queen Elizabeth granted it to Edward Carey who, in turn, passed it on to Sir John Savile, later Baron Savile of Pontefract. During the Civil War, Sandal Castle was garrisoned by the Royalists. But the Parliamentarians laid siege in the summer of 1645 and, after breaching the walls in several places with artillery bombardment, accepted the surrender of the castle on 30 September, though some sources say it held out until late October. The castle was later to suffer the same fate as Pontefract and other major Yorkshire fortresses, and this proud fortress was reduced to mere rubble.

Conisbrough Castle is said to boast the finest circular keep in England, both in terms of design and masonry. It was built by the de Warrennes, and its history is very similar to that of Sandal Castle, being part of the same estates. Conisbrough is fortunate in that the remains of its keep are in relatively good repair and the structure sound. In a county where many of the past's strongholds have been reduced to rubble, this fine castle stands yet proud and dominant over the terrain. It is little wonder then that Sir Walter Scott should have chosen Conisbrough Castle, and the neighbourhood of Rotherham, as the setting for the chief scenes of his novel *Ivanhoe*. The funeral feast described in Ivanhoe takes place within the keep at Conisbrough Castle, with another chamber also noted as the room where 'Rowena and her maidens sat working the silken pall', and the little chapel where 'the bier of Athelstane stood'.

Knaresborough Castle was retained in the King's hands after the Norman Conquest. It was to remain among the royal estates until 1372 when it was granted to John of Gaunt, Duke of Lancaster. Since then it has remained as part of the Duchy of Lancaster. The castle is significant for a number of minor episodes in the unfolding pageant of history. The four knights who murdered Thomas á Becket in Canterbury Cathedral sought refuge in Knaresborough Castle. They remained prisoners there for many months. Subsequently, they were pardoned on condition of their performing a pilgrimage to Jerusalem.

In 1318 the town of Knaresborough was burned and pillaged by the Scots, against which attack the castle could only offer a mere minimum of resistance, being garrisoned by only ten men-at-arms and thirty footmen. Richard II was imprisoned at Knaresborough during the year 1399 before being taken to Pontefract where he was to die. Legend has it that, during his stay in the castle, his captors deprived him of any sleep through relays of men who beat drums each time his eyes closed.

During the Civil War, Knaresborough was garrisoned for the King, but surrendered after a short siege of just over three weeks on 20 December 1644. Reports at the time claimed that: 'In the castle was found four pieces of fine ordnance; a large store of arms, powder and ammunition; a considerable quantity of specie and plate to the value of £1,500, with other valuable booty.' The castle was also demolished by order of Parliament for its support of the Royalist cause.

Clifford's Tower at York was built by Henry III. The site of the fortress, at the confluence of the rivers Ouse and Foss, had been recognised as a strong defensive position from Roman times and had boasted a number of previous structures. Clifford's Tower is situated on the east bank of the Ouse and was faced on the opposite bank by the Castle of Old Baile, which has by now almost completely disappeared.

The castle at York is connected with one particular and shameful incident concerning the Jews of York in 1190, during the reign of Richard I. At that time, a fanatical and bloodthirsty outbreak

A bird's-eye view of the striking Norman keep of Conisbrough Castle, overlooking the river Don. (Crown copyright reserved)

of fierce hatred of the Jews suddenly sprang up amongst the common people. The persecution of the Jews had started in London when Richard I, on the day before his coronation, had banned Jews from attendance at Westminster: 'lest he might suffer by their magical arts'. Some Jews had managed to be present at Westminster Hall and, when their presence was discovered, they were attacked and beaten. The violence at the royal court then quickly spread to the rest of the city. Many people in the city believed that the King had ordered the extermination of these Jewish settlers. Their houses were plundered, their possessions stolen, and many of those Jews who had barricaded themselves in their homes were burnt to death. Others were executed and their bodies thrown onto fires that had been kindled in the streets. 'The feeble, the sick and the dying' were treated likewise. The violence and massacres in London then spread to other towns and cities.

One account of what happened in York gives the following narrative of the events. The Jews of York, quite rightly fearing for their safety after the house of one of their number was burned by a vicious mob, sought refuge in the castle. The mob laid siege to Clifford's Tower, but all was secure inside until the governor of the fortress had occasion to leave the castle. On his return, the Jews feared that during his absence he might have turned against them, and so they refused him admittance. Enraged at this treatment, the governor sought permission from the high sheriff to besiege his own castle. The Jews, fearing the prospect of falling into the hands of the rabble, determined that they would sooner kill themselves than be foully treated and defiled by the mob. Some 500 Jews were to die this way by their own hands, or by some of their own number who were given the task of cutting the throats of others. Those Jews who decided that they would rather live and trust in the mercy of their enemies, opened the gates of the castle and, despite saying that they would become Christians, were attacked and cut to pieces by the mob.

However, the episode in York was described in another account as follows:

At York, the Jews took refuge in the castle; but unable to defend themselves, they shared the same or rather a worse fate than their brethren in the capital. The castle was besieged for several days. On the night before the expected assault, a rabbi, lately arrived from the Hebrew schools abroad, addressed his fellow countrymen in these words: 'Men of Israel! God commands us to die for his law, as our glorious forefathers have done in all ages. If we fall into the hands of our enemies they may cruelly torment us. That life which our Creator gave us, let us return to him willingly and devoutly with our own hands.' No sooner had the rabbi finished, than the men murdered their wives and children, threw the dead bodies over the walls on the populace; set fire to the building and perished in the flames. It is said that nearly 2,000 Jews in York alone fell victims to this sanguinary persecution.

Whichever account is accurate, it is clear that this persecution of the Jewish citizens in York was a shameful incident and horrific event. The Jews were expelled from England in 1290 by King Edward I and were not to be allowed back in England until 1656. However, the Jews did not return to the city of York. It was said that there was a curse on the city and Jews were not supposed to eat or spend the night there. It took centuries before the Jewish aversion and antipathy to York was ended. In 1990 the Chief Rabbi of England and the Archbishop of York held a joint ceremony of reconciliation at Clifford's Tower and a service of forgiveness and reparation.

The quatrefoil keep, known as Clifford's Tower, was only the second of this type of fortress to be built in England. The other example was at Pontefract, also engineered by Henry III. The origin of the name Clifford probably commemorates one Sir Robert Clifford, who was executed for his part in the rising of 1322, and whose body was hung in chains from the summit of the tower. From this time on the castle was allowed to fall into neglect, until the time of the Civil War when it was repaired, strengthened, and armed with cannon. It withstood a very long siege against the Parliamentarians but inevitably had to yield and surrender to the Roundhead army. The end of York Castle came on the night of 23 April 1684 when a fire, which started in Clifford's Tower, spread to a powder magazine resulting in as violent explosion so severe as to leave only the outer walls standing, as a picturesque ruin.

The other Yorkshire castles, notably Richmond, Scarborough, Sheffield, Skipton, Tickhill, Bowes, Helmsley and Middleham have their own particular tales to tell. Lesser-known and more obscure castles – for example, Kippax, Northallerton, Sheriff Hutton, Tadcaster, Thorne and Sedbergh – have also had their moments. Without doubt these places and the incidents connected with them, merit further explorations. Their ruins and sites endure and remain to be visited. Their stories can be discovered and relived from a host of sources. 'Our histories are full of Pontefract Castle', wrote Swift. Sad indeed is the plight of this fortress, foremost of all the castles in the county. Some ruins do remain; a little of the structure still stands as a constant reminder to a modern world of times past when chivalry, honour, valour and feats of strength at arms were the predominant values. Fortunately our history is only scantily covered with the passing of time: its true story is easily unfolded and explored by those who are prepared to take the time and trouble to do so.

Chapter Four

Yorkshire Abbeys

Yorkshire as a county is particularly well-endowed with a number of fine examples and monuments of an earlier time when the dual power of the Church and the Crown were the over-riding authorities in the lives of all men. This partnership in the affairs of men was not to last. The Church and the State were separated by the rift between King and Pope, which was sparked off by the sovereign's marital problems. The row that led to the Reformation was to cause a revolution in the economy and society of the country as well as in the religious aspects of life.

The Church has been criticised for maintaining the feudal system and for producing a stagnant society that resisted any attempts at change, new ideas or reform. When the Reformation came, it marked not only a radical change in the position of the Church and the clergy in the scheme of government, but a more fundamental change of attitudes and ideas in the minds of some men. Men who were more prepared to challenge the assumptions of authority and replace new faiths for old. The zeal of the new faith, however, rigorously destroyed the vestiges of the old. Systematically, the marks of Catholicism were removed from the countryside.

The monasteries and abbeys that were built in the county of Yorkshire were without doubt among the finest of their kind built anywhere in the Christian world. Their loss is all the more regrettable since the remnants and ruins that are still extant serve to echo their past glory and former magnificence. These former splendid edifices have been left to the ravages of time and have fallen into ruin since the irascible, jealous, greedy and resentful Henry VIII ordered the Dissolution of minor monasteries in 1536 and of the major monastic establishments in 1539.

Monasticism had been a recurring feature in ecclesiastical life from the very early origins of the Christian faith. However, it was not until the sixth century that any lasting attempt was made to organise and discipline the monastic life. Too many of the early monasteries were merely groups of hermits who were reluctant to settle in any one place for any length of time. The strength of purpose of these early ascetics was also subject to occasional lapses.

This pattern of early monastic life was to change with the work of one Benedict of Nursia, born in AD 480. Benedict left home at the tender age of fourteen and moved to Subiaco, not far from Rome, where he lived in a cave as a hermit for three years. A neighbouring monastery then elected him as their abbot. Benedict gave up his life of solitude and devoted himself to his new position as head of this community of monks. His predecessor had let the life of the abbey fall into a very relaxed state but, as the new abbot, Benedict was determined to alter this. Benedict's rule proved far too strict for many of his subjects who had grown accustomed to the easy life and, at one stage, they even tried to poison his food in order to be rid of this zealous reformer. At this point, Benedict resigned his position and decided to set up his own monastery at Monte Cassino in about AD 540. This was the birth of the new Benedictine rule. The *Regula Monachorum* became the basis of the rule of all Western Christian monastic orders. (The Benedictines are perhaps better known today for the liqueur that they made from a secret recipe, which was invented and developed at the monastery of Fécamp, in France, in about 1510.)

The rules for monastic life that Benedict demanded from all the monks at Monte Cassino quickly spread as a new force in the Christian world. Hundreds of new establishments were built throughout Europe. All of them deriving their pattern of life from the parent foundation of Monte Cassino, and all strictly adhering to the Benedictine rule. Benedict was concerned with introducing a more vigorous monastic life into the older foundations whose discipline had become disgracefully relaxed. Benedictine rule was to be a fuller, more disciplined and perfect monasticism. Hence, not only were new monasteries founded but many of those already existing were pulled down and rebuilt to adapt to the requirements of the new rule.

These new monasteries would all follow the same basic plan, though some modifications were often necessary to accommodate local circumstances and geography. The Benedictine establishment, wherever possible, should contain within itself every necessity of life, as well as the buildings more intimately connected with the religious and social life of its inmates. The plan, which was meant to be repeated within all foundations, included provision for bake-houses, stables, dormitories, storehouses, cloisters, a chapter house, kitchens, an infirmary, as well as a church and a chapel to meet the requirements of the religious contemplative life. The Benedictine community was designed to be a self-contained and self-supporting community, with as little reliance and contact with the outside world as possible. This was to be the pattern of monastic life for centuries to come. Exceptions were made for those monks who were to deal directly with the general public and community such as almoners, healers and porters.

The spread of Christianity and monasticism reached the shores of England via St Columba and the community of monks he established on the island of Iona, and also through the actions of St Bede, who inaugurated a similar community at Jarrow on the banks of the Tyne. The peoples in these Celtic fringes of Europe were gradually converted to the new Christian beliefs, and before too long the monastery became an accepted and regular feature of the English countryside. In these early years, the monastic foundations flourished and began to assume great importance in the everyday life of the peasants of Northumbria. The monasteries offered shelter for the traveller, alms for the poor, treatment for the sick and the infirm, and the beginnings of an education for a fortunate few. But by the tenth century, during a period of history often described as the Dark Ages, the significance of the monastery had declined, and monasticism was at its lowest ebb.

This situation of monastic decline may be attributed to three main causes. First, the raids and attacks by marauding Northmen severely harassed the monastic settlements. Secondly, the growth of the feudal system had converted many of the abbots into powerful secular lords by virtue of the holdings of land that the monasteries possessed. Thirdly, monastic incomes and revenues had often been seized or appropriated by kings, princes and bishops. The effects of this decline in the incidence of monastic life were more severe in the North than in the South. The attacks by the Danes and Vikings and the laying waste of Northumbria left only a few remaining monasteries. Those that did survive were generally possessed by married clergy. Christianity became almost extinct and very few churches were built or rebuilt. No new monasteries were founded for nearly 200 years. The country people never heard the name of a monk and were frightened by the very sight of a monastic habit.

The revival of the monasteries in the North was partly due to the migration of certain monks from the South, which had been relatively isolated from persecution at the hands of the invading Vikings. Three monks, in particular, left Evesham in 1073 and moved to a site on the River Tyne. After some time, the three separated. Aldwin went to Durham, Rienefried went to Whitby and Elfwin moved to York where he began working to restore the monastery which was dedicated to St Mary.

St Mary's Abbey, York, had been founded on the site of an earlier church named Galmanho, which was built in honour of St Olaf. Earl (or Jarl) Siward had erected the church in his capital to revere St Olaf who, by this time, 'was dearly loved by all men of Scandinavian descent'. It was this church of St Olaf, together with the surrounding plot of some four acres of land, that was to grow into the noble abbey of St Mary immediately after the Norman Conquest. Under the leadership of Elfwin, the Abbey at York quickly developed into a new centre of monasticism in the North. St Mary's adopted the strict Benedictine rule, but later abbots were lacking in their application of rules, and the internal discipline of the community became scandalously lax.

Part of the reason for this lay with the site of the abbey. The growth of York into the major ecclesiastical, political and military centre outside London, and its important role as capital of the North, meant that the abbey's position in the city increased in importance, prestige and value. Moreover, the quality and extent of the abbey's lands outside the city gave considerable

Whitby graveyard.

temporal power to the abbot. A quarrel began with one Thomas de Warthill over the disputed ownership of a slice of the abbey lands. This dispute was only settled by the direct intervention of the King, who found in favour of de Warthill and accordingly fined the abbey heavily. This almost caused the financial ruin and collapse of the abbey, but with time prosperity returned to the monks.

The lifestyle and general prosperity enjoyed by the abbot and monks of St Mary's was the cause of a later series of troubles at the hands of the citizens of York, who became jealous and angry at the monastery's privileges and wealth. Frequent clashes and collisions between monks and citizens occurred until 1262 when an attack on the monastery resulted in much damage to property and loss of life. The enmity was finally ended by a settlement by the abbot of a significant sum of money as a peace offering.

The lack of discipline in the monastery at York caused a schism amongst its members in 1132, when a group of thirteen monks, including the prior, Richard, decided to leave in order to found a new community based on the Cistercian reform of the Benedictine rule. The foundation that they began became the fourth Cistercian abbey in the history of English monasticism, famous in its own right as the beautiful Fountains Abbey.

By the time of the Dissolution in 1536, the community at St Mary's was probably in the order of 150 members. The revenue of the establishment is estimated to have been £2,000 a year, which would be a very large amount for those days. The last abbot of St Mary's was named

Fountains Abbey, near Ripon, an outstanding piece of Yorkshire's heritage and the best preserved Cistercian Monastery in Britain.

Thornton and, on surrendering the monastery and its revenue to the Crown, he received a pension of 400 marks. (A mark was then worth about two-thirds of a pound sterling.) The abbey was retained by the Crown, but the buildings were allowed to fall into disrepair. In 1701 the site was partly demolished for stone to build the county gaol, and royal grants of stone were further given in 1705 and 1717 for the repair of St Olave's Church and Beverley Minster respectively.

Rievaulx Abbey was founded in 1131 and was the first of the Cistercian order of monasteries to be built in the North of England. Waverley in Surrey founded in 1128, and Tintern Abbey founded in 1131, were the first two Cistercian abbeys to be built in England. It is significant that the next two abbeys to be built were Rievaulx and Fountains, both in the county of Yorkshire, which was already rich in abbeys and priories by that time.

The Cistercians, also called the White Monks, had originated from Citeaux. The order was founded in 1098, under the guidance of St Bernard. It was Bernard who introduced a new vigour into the well-established Benedictine rule that had lapsed into a contemptible state. The Cistercian reform emphasised the barest simplicity in life. The dangers of seeking or valuing 'art for its own sake' had meant that the monasteries were becoming more and more concerned with the beauty and value of 'products of art' rather than concentrating on contemplation and meditating on the laws of God. The Cistercian order reacted strongly against this secularisation and laxity. The new Cistercian rule was determined to concentrate

One of the most picturesquely sited of Yorkshire's monasteries is Rievaulx Abbey, in the wooded valley of the river Wye. (Bertram Unne)

exclusively on spiritual matters and was prepared to devote only the absolute minimum of time to the furtherance of temporal affairs.

The Cistercian monastery at Rievaulx owes its origins to Sir Walter l'Espec, the Lord of Helmsley. He gave an area of land in the valley of the River Rye to a group of monks from Citeaux, so that they might settle and build a religious house there. Sir Walter had lost his favourite son, who had broken his neck when thrown from his horse, and he was anxious to commemorate the unfortunate youth. The settlement that the Cistercians built up became known as Rievaulx, taking its name from nearby Ryevale. Sir Walter, who had been a notable warrior and had figured largely in the Battle of the Standard, later gave up his former life and became a monk in the very abbey that he had been so instrumental in founding. He finished his life as a serving monk within the walls of Rievaulx and was buried in the chapter house in 1153.

The site of the new abbey at Rievaulx did not permit following the exact building plan as laid down in the rules of the order. Contrary to the usual practice, the arms of the church were not orientated to the cardinal points of the compass. The traditional pattern was to build the church in a typical cruciform shape, with the nave running from east to west, the chancel pointing due east, and with the transepts built at right angles to the nave and running north to south. In Rievaulx, the nave of the church, the largest Cistercian nave in England, ran almost north to south. Apart from this change in general orientation, the remainder of the abbey follows very closely the recurrent and regimented pattern of that time. Like the earlier Benedictine settlements, the community was purpose built and so designed in order to contain and provide for all the material and temporal needs of its members.

The life of the abbey since its foundation was without any serious incident. It seems to have been relatively free from the problems of raids and other disturbances until its suppression during the Reformation. The monastery was surrendered by Abbot Richard de Blyton after four centuries of peaceful monastic life. Abbot de Blyton and the few monks remaining at the time of the Dissolution did receive some small compensation for their loss, but the buildings and estates passed to the Earl of Rutland. The monastery fell into disuse as a centre of religious worship. Naught but a few ruins of the structure are left behind today to give an indication of its former function and importance.

Fountains Abbey, situated near Ripon, was the second Cistercian foundation to be established in Yorkshire. It was started by a breakaway group of twelve monks who, under Prior Richard, had left St Mary's in York in search of a more strenuous and disciplined religious life. They decided after consultation with their archbishop to found a community of their own, adopting the Cistercian reforms of the earlier Benedictine rule. The archbishop sent the monks to Ripon and while there they determined on a site in Skelldale as the spot to build their new community and settlement. The conditions of the site were described as wretched. The land was wild and uncultivated, and was said to be 'more suited for the haunts of wild beasts than the abode of man.' In spite of these natural deprivations, the small body of brothers set about clearing the land and quarrying stone to begin their mammoth task.

There is a local legend, about the early days of the building of the monastery, that readily shows the simple faith of these monks. The monks had only bread for food and for drink they only had water from the river. A traveller passing by stopped at the site and begged for food from the poverty-stricken community. The abbot was consulted about the beggar's request and, on discovering that there were only two and a half loaves of bread left, he ordered that the beggar be given one of the loaves, leaving the rest to be shared by the workmen. As for the future, he said, 'The Lord will provide'. Later that day, an unexpected and opportune gift was received from Eustace Fitz-John of Knaresborough who, out of kindness, had ordered that a whole load of bread be delivered to the monks at his expense. It seemed that the Lord had indeed provided, and no further incentive was needed by the community to ensure that all worked to full capacity to complete the task of building the new monastery.

From these humble beginnings the monastic community at Fountains soon prospered and, despite the original hardships and difficult conditions, the community was soon rewarded for its effort and hard work. Throughout the centuries the territory of the abbey increased. Its revenues were calculated to be almost £1,000 a year by the time of its Dissolution in 1536. Perhaps more impressive was the number of animals that the monks tended on the pastures that they had created from the surrounding hills. By the time of the Reformation, the abbey had flocks of 1,000 sheep and twice as many cattle, 100 horses, and almost as many pigs. This was a far cry indeed from the small company of monks under the leadership of Prior Richard that had braved the wilderness and harsh winters in those early days of foundation.

Jervaulx Abbey was founded in 1156 by a company of Cistercian monks who had left the abbey of Byland in order to start their own colony. This group of monks had tried to establish a community in 1150 at Fors, near Askrigg, under John de Kingston as abbot. However, the site at Fors was not entirely suitable for a religious house: the soil was poor, the climate bleak and

The imposing remains of Fountains Abbey.

Byland Abbey.

the landscape inhospitable and open to the full force of the wind and weather. For five years the monks struggled against the harshness and deprivations of this environment and they were often reduced to little more than starvation. The Earl of Richmond took pity on this noble band of men and granted them new lands at East Witton in 1156, which were far more suitable for their intended settlement.

The monks chose as the site to build their church and other monastic buildings a delightful spot close by the River Ure, which contained a considerable amount of rich water meadow and pasture at the bottom of the valley. It was also surrounded by green and fertile hills. The monastery built in this very quiet and restful locale continued in wealth and prosperity from the time of its foundation, until it too shared the common fate of English monasteries and was confiscated by King Henry VIII. The King ordered that all the lead be removed from the roof and that the fabric should be ransacked for anything of value. After this, the walls were demolished and the once noble building decayed into rubble, with the exception of a few arches and fragments of wall.

The severity that the King showed in his treatment of Jervaulx is partly to be explained by the actions of the last abbot, Adam Sedbergh. At the time of the Dissolution, the abbot was prepared to surrender Jervaulx to the Crown, but the local people were incensed by the King's actions and demanded that the abbot and the abbey resist the avaricious Henry. The abbot was persuaded to change his mind, partly by threats on his life. He also took action against the King in the rising known as the Pilgrimage of Grace in 1537. This rebellion, led by Robert Aske, a Yorkshire gentleman, might have had some chance of success had not its leaders been so easily placated by the King.

The rebels commanded as many as 40,000 men under their standard. Aske's rebels soon captured York, Pontefract and Hull. For a time, the city of York remained in the hands of Aske and his followers, and York became a centre to which dispossessed monks and friars were invited to be 'reinstated'. Before too long, a royal army appeared at York. At first sight, it seemed scarcely sufficient to deal with the rebellion, but the King's generals were able to dissuade the rebels from further action by making a host of promises of fair treatment and the rising quietly died down.

Far too readily, the rebels accepted a host of compromises and reforms that Henry immediately retracted when the insurrection died down. Given Henry's past actions, this failure to keep his word is hardly surprising, but the rebels took the King's word of honour. All the key men in the revolt, including the abbot Adam Sedbergh, were taken prisoner and later executed. The unfortunate abbot was imprisoned in the Tower of London and subsequently hanged at Tyburn. His was an ironic fate, as he had taken part in the mutiny for 'fear of reprisals otherwise, and still he suffered the same end.' Other rebels from the Pilgrimage of Grace also paid a heavy cost for their part in the revolt. Public executions took place in every market town from Wetherby to Newcastle, and 'great severity was shown to the other prisoners who escaped the headman's axe'.

Bolton Priory stands in a secluded spot in the valley of the Wharfe. The story of its foundation goes back to a company of Augustinian monks at Embsay, two miles east of Skipton, which was dedicated to the honour of the Virgin Mary and St Cuthbert. The tradition behind the migration of these monks from Embsay to Bolton is told in the legend of Romilly, the boy of Egremond. The story is also the subject of a verse by Wordsworth.

The legend is generally told as follows. Not far from Bolton the River Wharfe winds its way through the woods along the valley until suddenly the waters reach a natural constriction in the river bed where the river is reduced in width to a mere 4ft. As a consequence of this restriction in the flow of the water, the river has cut a deep narrow chasm in the rock floor. This place, known as the Strid, has for centuries attracted people of all ages to risk its very real dangers by jumping across the river in defiance of 'the destruction that awaits the faltering step'. One day a young boy named Romilly, heir to the lands around Bolton, was out hunting with his greyhound in the woods when he came upon the Strid. He attempted to jump across it, just as he had done many times before. But the dog, instead of leaping with him, 'held back and checked its master in his flight'. Romilly, still holding the dog's leash, fell short of the bank, disappeared into the swirling rapids and was drowned. The dog too fell into the water, but was more fortunate and survived. The accident was witnessed by a forester, who set off at once to find the boy's mother and relate the sad tale. Understandably heartbroken by the news, the boy's mother, Alicia, decided to perpetuate her son's memory by dedicating the land around Bolton to the monks of Embsay. The monks built their priory at the nearest site possible to the place of the boy's mishap. Thus in 1154, the Augustinian monks began to construct their priory which, on completion, must surely have ranked as amongst the most beautiful and magnificent of its kind.

After four centuries of peaceful existence, this monastery too was surrendered to the King. Like Jervaulx, the priory of Bolton was also connected with the Pilgrimage of Grace in 1537, via the Norton family, some of whom were executed for their part as prominent participants and leaders in the mutiny. One of the Nortons, named Francis, was killed by a troop of the King's Horse near his home at Rylstone, not far from Bolton. This Francis Norton had given his younger sister Emily a present of a beautiful white fawn. After the burial of Francis in the priory grounds at Bolton, Emily would often bring her pet deer with her when she came to mourn at her brother's tomb. The girl is said to have died of grief at her brother's death and the young deer, now alone, refused to leave the priory or the graves of Francis and Emily. The spirits of Emily and the small deer are still said to be seen constantly in the vicinity of the priory and the ruined church.

Kirkstall Abbey, situated on the outskirts of Leeds, owes its origins to Henry de Lacy of Pontefract. Henry, after recovering from a protracted and serious illness, kept his solemn vow that, if he were to be spared from death, he would erect an abbey for the Cistercian monks. Henry originally assigned lands at Barnoldswick for the site of the monastery, but this settlement was troubled by raiding Scots who robbed the monks of the little they had. Alexander, the abbot, then decided to change the location and searched the countryside for a site for the new retreat. Eventually, he determined on a site at Kirkstall in Airedale, which was already inhabited by a few hermits. Henry de Lacy was consulted about the new site and it was he who obtained from William de Poitou, the owner of the surrounding lands, a grant to build a new monastery in 1153. Henry de Lacy was indeed generous as the abbey's patron and he bore the whole expense of the construction of Kirkstall.

John Ripley was the last abbot at Kirkstall. He surrendered the monastery to the Crown at the Dissolution. After three years it was granted to Thomas Cranmer, Archbishop of Canterbury, who settled the property on his younger son. During those three years, the roof was taken off the church, the bells removed from the tower, and the buildings rendered uninhabitable by the removal of lead and timber, all of which was sold for the benefit of the royal purse.

The other notable abbeys of Yorkshire, such as Roche, Byland, Whitby, Mount Grace, Richmond, Kirkham and Easby all suffered similar fates. The force of monasticism was eradicated from the Yorkshire countryside, but its traces still remain in the many ruins and fragments left standing on the sites of these former houses of contemplation and worship. By the end of the Dissolution:

> Henry VIII suppressed in England and Wales, 643 monasteries, 90 colleges, 2,374 churches and chapels, and 110 hospitals and had the abbots of Reading, Glastonbury, and St John's Colchester, hanged and quartered, for refusing to surrender their abbeys, and for denying his supremacy.

Many of the monasteries had grown rich since their foundation and, in some instances, religious fervour had been lost as a consequence of the pursuit of material wealth, power and selfish gain. Some abbots were indeed powerful temporal lords of some affluence and political standing, instead of being spiritual leaders practising humility and asceticism. Even so, the contribution that the abbeys made to the development of the nation and their legacy, which is still apparent today, should not be demeaned or underestimated.

The monasteries provided poor relief long before the days of the poor law. Apart from this, the monks and monasteries ministered to the sick, and they were also the only source of care available for orphans. The monks often provided a means of education for the common people that was unobtainable elsewhere. It is true that the monasteries grew wealthy, but this was a direct consequence of their own hard work. Their motto was *laborare est orare* – to work is to pray. It was this very attitude to work, and the sweated labour of monks dedicated to the service

Kirkstall Abbey on the outskirts of Leeds.

of God that, coupled with a doctrine of asceticism, provided the prosperity and wealth of the monasteries that proved in the end to be their downfall.

Yorkshire, in particular, owes a special debt of gratitude to the monasticism that once graced its lands. The influence of the monastery extended far outside the religious sphere. The monks introduced an element of 'scientific' agriculture for those times. They drained fens and swamps, cleared forests, built roads, and were the architects and builders of extremely durable structures. It was also the religious settlements throughout the county that were first responsible for the development of the woollen industry, an industry which has played a decisive part, not only in the industrial development of the county, but also in the economic and social history of the nation. It was the early monastic settlements who first introduced sheep to reclaimed pastures, and this paved the way for a new agriculture.

The sheer beauty of many of the former monastic sites is almost entirely due to the work of the monks and the monasteries themselves. Very often, the sites on which the monastic communities were founded could hardly be described as habitable or welcoming. It was only in opposition to severe, adverse geographical and physical conditions that the wilderness was tamed and converted into the picturesque and scenic places that they are today.

Chapter Five

Historic York

The city of York, from very early times, has been closely connected with many major national events. To know the story of York is also to know much of English history. York is in many ways unequalled by any other city in the kingdom. The medieval character of the city is still apparent to the modern visitor. Its many narrow streets, medieval churches, quaint buildings, imposing gateways, city walls and ramparts, the magnificent Minster, have been relatively little affected by the passing of time. This is in contrast to many other cities whose historical inheritance and present architecture only very scantily reflect former importance, structures, fortifications and fine buildings. Other towns and cities do have characteristic features and advantages peculiar to themselves, but York has a charm and attraction all of its own. This charm lies in the sense of history so easily realised from the many fine examples of a much chequered past: a notion of history reinforced by a wealth of monuments, buildings and churches of bygone days.

Historical relics and remains by themselves can only give some impressions of life in earlier times. In York, the all-pervading character of the city builds on these impressions and rouses the imagination to think of the past. For example, to see York as a Roman town strongly fortified and garrisoned by the famous Sixth Legion, or as the Viking settlement of Jorvik, or as a bustling medieval city and port – or perhaps even as a defiant and proud Royalist stronghold under siege from a determined Parliamentarian army vainly trying to breach the city walls with artillery bombardments. York has been prominent in ecclesiastical, military and civil affairs since very early times. York was the centre of almost all the chief events in the North of England up to the time of the Civil War. Although its importance in national affairs has declined since then, it is this former prominence that explains the development of the city and its gradual expansions from an early settlement into a busy city and port of Stuart times.

Before the Roman invasions of England, a tribe of Celtic peoples known as the Brigantes had formed a settlement on an island at the junction of the rivers Ouse and Foss. This small settlement became known as Eburach, which is understood to mean 'the field at the meeting of the waters'. The Brigantes were not an homogenous group of peoples, but were composed of many small tribes, and were generally quite fierce and warlike. Their settlement at Eburach developed quite quickly on account of its central position, its fairly easy access to the sea via a navigable river, and its proximity to one of the major north-south natural road-tracks of the time.

To the north of Eburach stretched a vast dense forest, later known as the Forest of Galtres. To the east, the land was low-lying and often swamp-like, being particularly prone to floods. Eburach was especially well placed for these early lines of communication across a hostile countryside whose forests and swamps made travelling especially hazardous.

Although the Romans invaded the south of England in 55 BC, the conquest of the north and of the Brigantes did not begin until AD 70. Britain at this time was described as 'being occupied by barbarous tribes who lived upon animals caught in hunting and on fruits and plants. They stained and tattooed their bodies and wore personal ornaments and trinkets made of iron. They had no religion but a bloody idolatry called Druidism.'

The Roman army and legions, under the generalship of Julius Agricola, originally used Aldborough as their headquarters during their campaigns in the North. However, in AD 80 Agricola moved his headquarters to Eburach to take advantage of the natural defensive position offered by a site flanked by deep navigable waters. The Roman occupation forces built a camp at Eburach, after their own very characteristic style, in the form of huge rectangle with a gate in the middle of each of the four walls. This camp was fortified by digging deep trenches and using the earth to build ramparts. In later years a wall was built round the camp and towers were added at each corner to increase the defences even further. Thus the Romans created a military capital in the North of Britain, which became known as Eboracum.

Of the Roman camp at Eboracum sufficient traces of the original walls remain, demonstrating fairly accurately the extent of this military centre. At the north-west corner the Roman tower built to protect the camp is well preserved in places, and is known as the Multangular Tower because of its many sides and angles. Under the Roman occupation several roads were built, the river at York was bridged, and many fine stone houses replaced the older, cruder wooden buildings of Eburach.

Hadrian was the first Roman Emperor to visit Eboracum. In AD 121 Hadrian began the construction of a fortified wall between the Tyne and the Solway Firth to keep the Picts and the Scots at bay. Hadrian also sent the Sixth Legion to Eboracum, where it was to be stationed for the next three hundred years. The Emperor Severus was next to visit the Roman military capital of the North. Severus was engaged in many campaigns against the Scots until his death at the age of seventy-three in AD 211. He was buried outside the city walls on a hill that is still known as Severus Hill. Constantine the Great became Emperor in AD 306 and was the first Christian Emperor of Rome. His father had spent a number of years at Eboracum during many visits and had finally died there.

By this time, Eboracum was at the height of its glory. No other city in the Roman provinces in the west could compare with it. Many villas and palaces had been built for the Roman nobility that had settled there, and numerous temples had been dedicated to the gods. This golden age was not to last indefinitely. Barbarian invasions were threatening the Empire and, as a consequence, in AD 410 the Roman legions were withdrawn from Britain. Britain was now left defenceless, a prey to plunderers and marauders from overseas.

Eboracum was attacked on many occasions, from the north by the Picts and by sea-raiders from the Continent, especially Angles and Saxons from the basins of the Elbe. The Brigantes treated Eboracum as a haven, a place of safety and retreat from the many invaders that came after the Roman withdrawal in search of booty and plunder. The city became known by the Celtic name, *Caer-Ebrauc*, the word 'caer' meaning a place of safety. Eventually, the invading

Angles overcame the Celtic resistance. The plain of York was over-run and the area developed into the Anglian province of Deira.

In the seventh century, the Anglian King Edwin united the province of Deira with the neighbouring province to the north known as Bernicia. The combined lands, stretching from the Humber to the Firth of Forth, were renamed Northumbria. Eoferwick, the Anglian name for Eboracum, became the capital of Northumbria which, at that time, was the leading power in the country. King Edwin had married Ethelburga, daughter of Ethelbert, King of Kent. It was Ethelburga who brought Paulinus to Eoferwick from Kent as her chaplain. St Paulinus was made the first bishop of Northumbria and, during the long and peaceful reign of Edwin, the country experienced a time of peace and order unknown since the departure of the Romans. Eoferwick became a centre of religion. Later, from the time of Archbishop Egbert (732–766), it also became celebrated as a place of learning. Under Alcuin, the city became known as one of the foremost places of education in Europe.

At the beginning of the ninth century, another wave of attackers began to raid and pillage the coasts of Northern England. These marauders came in long narrow ships, which drew very little water and, therefore, could sail far inland up the creeks and rivers. Danish (or Viking) plunderers had come from across the North Sea, as the Angles had also done, but these latest invaders had come from farther north. The Danes captured Eoferwick in AD 867 and the town was given the Viking name of Jorvik. Jorvik quickly became one of the principal Danish settlements and seats of commerce and trade. By AD 990 its population was estimated to have been 30,000. Northumbria formed one of the Danish Jarldoms and Jorvik became the capital of Northumbria. The most famous of the Danish Jarls who lived at Jorvik was Siward, who died in 1055. It is reputed that Siward on his deathbed insisted on being clothed in his armour and helmet and, in this way he died, propped up in his bed while dressed as a warrior and still grasping his mighty battle-axe.

After the death of Edward the Confessor, Harold Godwin, the Earl of Wessex, was declared King of England. Harold's outlawed brother Tostig joined forces with Harald Hardrada, the King of Norway. Together, with a vast fleet of ships, they set sail from Norway with the intention of invading England and seizing the land for themselves. The invading fleet sailed up the Humber, landed at Riccall, marched on York and captured the city. King Harold, in the south of England at the time, heard of the invasion and hurried north to meet the threat. On 25 September 1066, Harold and his Saxon army defeated the Danes at the Battle of Stamford Bridge. The Danish army was put to flight, and much of the fleet destroyed before the retreating Danes could sail away to safety. Of the vast armada that had set out to invade England only a handful of ships returned. Unfortunately for Harold, it was during the triumphant victory feast at York following the battle that news came that the Normans, under Duke William, had landed.

William the Conqueror quickly overran the South of England after his victory at Hastings. However, the North, including the city of York due to its strong Danish influence, stubbornly resisted the Norman invaders. William came north in 1068 and captured York, which showed surprisingly little resistance. William built a tower to guard the city, left a garrison of five hundred men in command, and departed for the south. Almost as soon as he had gone, the garrison was attacked and struggled to hold out until William could return with a relieving force. So William built a second, much stronger castle and this time left behind a strengthened garrison of 3,000 men.

In the following year, 1069, a fleet of Danish longships sailed up the Ouse and, together with the citizens of York, attacked the Norman fortress and captured the city. The surviving Norman garrison was, without exception, put to the sword. The enraged William, on receiving news of this disaster, quickly marched north again. Only after a long siege was he able to recapture the city. By now William had lost all patience with the people of the North and was determined to put an end to these rebellions. He ordered that the North of England should be 'wasted'. The countryside was put to the flame, many of the peasants were killed, and the houses and towns were destroyed. As a consequence, Yorkshire and Durham were left desolated and it was to take almost a century before the North fully recovered from this devastation.

The first Parliament to be mentioned by that name in British history was held at York in 1160 by Henry II, when Malcolm, King of Scotland did homage for the territories he held as a vassal of the King of England. York once again assumed great importance as the capital of the North. Its position was well-fitted for its role as a military centre, not only because of the necessity to watch over the Borders, but also the sovereign was convinced that some kind of close royal supervision over the north was essential. Later rulers were to accept this situation and York retained its importance as a stronghold and fortress in command of the whole of the northern lands.

In 1322, Edward II used York as his headquarters both before and after the Battle of Boroughbridge, when the rebellion led by the Earl of Lancaster was put down. During the reign of Edward III in 1346, whilst the King and the Black Prince were fully engaged with the war in France, the Scots under David II invaded the North and actually burnt some of the suburbs of the city of York. Archbishop Zouche quickly assembled an army and marched northwards after the Scots, who had leisurely departed for their own country. The Scots, much to their surprise, were overtaken and defeated in a short encounter at Neville's Cross near Durham. King David II was taken captive and brought back to York before being taken south.

The city of York also played an important part in the struggles for the throne, now generally known as the War of the Roses. The citizens of York, however, did not support the White Rose but were strong supporters of the House of Lancaster. York became a centre and rallying point for the Lancastrian cause. Richard of York was killed at the Battle of Wakefield in 1460 and his army completely routed. The victorious Lancastrians found the bodies of the Duke of York and his son among the dead on the battlefield, and the heads of the duke and his son were removed and taken to York where they were exposed to view and openly displayed on the city walls.

York was further involved in rebellion and insurrection in 1536. Robert Aske, a Yorkshire gentleman, led a revolt known as the 'Pilgrimage of Grace' as a reaction to the dissolution of the monasteries ordered by Henry VIII. The uprising was defused by Henry with promises of safe passage made to the rebels, but these assurances proved false. Robert Aske, as ringleader, and the other leaders responsible for the rising were later executed for their audacity.

A similar rising and rebellion took place in 1569 when the Earls of Northumberland and Westmorland attempted to restore the Roman Catholic religion and Mary, Queen of Scots, to the throne. This rebellion, styled 'The Rising of the North', began well with the capture of Durham and from there an assault was launched on York, the rebels taking Darlington, Richmond, Ripon and Wetherby *en route*. Before reaching York, the Earl of Sussex with 5,000 men intercepted the rebels and very soon put the Earls and their rebellious army to flight. Westmorland escaped but Northumberland, after two year's sanctuary in Scotland, was given up to justice. He was beheaded on 22 August 1572 on a scaffold at York, and his head exposed for two years on Micklegate Bar. Another historical source, however, claims that the head of the Earl of Northumberland was mysteriously stolen during the night from Micklegate Bar sometime in 1573. (The city of York, apparently, also experienced a 'considerable earthquake' in the same year.)

During the Civil War, the city of York was again to play a major part in the nation's affairs. The county was mainly Royalist, although some of the most famous Parliamentarian officers were Yorkshiremen, among the most notable were Fairfax and Lambert. Charles I had moved to York from London in order to escape the growing climate of criticism there. York became the city of refuge for the persecuted King. Charles was dissuaded from making his headquarters at York, as many of the citizens feared attack from nearby Hull which had proved disloyal to the Royalist cause and strongly supported the Parliamentarians. The King left York for Nottingham and, on 22 August 1642, the King raised his royal standard, and the rift and rupture between King and Parliament was irrevocably beyond repair.

Fairfax laid siege to York in April 1644 but Prince Rupert, a brilliant tactician, was able to relieve the city after almost three months of blockade through a clever series of manoeuvres. Prince Rupert decided to press the matter and offered battle to the Roundhead army. The ensuing conflict at Marston Moor on 2 July 1644 proved disastrous to the hitherto invincible Rupert. The Royalist infantry was destroyed almost completely, and the cavalry left in a state of chaotic disorder. The Parliamentarian force grudgingly acknowledged admiration for the courage and tenacity of the Royalist forces which had fought so bitterly against the 'Ironsides' long after the day was all too obviously lost. Rupert managed to escape with almost 6,000 of his cavalry but was unable to return to York to save the city. The garrison came under siege again but by 16 July the city agreed to an honourable surrender, recognising that defeat was inevitable. The garrison was given an escort to Skipton which was still in Royalist hands. The city of York was saved from the disastrous effects of a long and severe bombardment.

This event was to prove the last major episode that the city of York would play in the political and monarchical history of the nation. York's future prominence was to be in other areas and activities.

The city walls were much damaged and battered during the siege of 1644 and later underwent some reconstruction and repair. Generally, the city walls are in a remarkably good state of preservation and large portions are still left standing, apparently little disturbed. Certain sections have been rebuilt and maintained on a number of occasions quite apart from the effects of the Civil War.

Chapter Six

York Minster is on Fire!

The Minster at York, in its present form, was built over a period of 250 years from the thirteenth to the fifteenth century. It is the fifth church to stand on the site. The original church was built of wood in AD 627 for the baptism of King Edwin. Edwin began building a stone church to replace the wooden structure, but this was not completed until after his death, and King Oswald finished the task in AD 641. In 1070 to 1100, Archbishop Thomas of Bordeaux began the construction of a Norman Minster, which at the time was the largest in England and possibly in Europe. Unfortunately, most of this building was destroyed by a disastrous fire in 1137. Archbishop Roger was responsible for rebuilding parts of the burnt-out Minster in 1154–1181, and remains of this church, the fourth Minster, can be seen in the crypt.

A corner of old York, with the east window of the Minster on the left, the Chapter House in the centre and St William's College on the right.

The present Minster was rededicated to St Peter on 3 February 1472, although it was not entirely completed by then. The building had taken two and a half centuries to finish from the construction of the south and north transepts from 1220–1260. The south-west tower was added in 1465, the north-west tower in 1474, and the central tower was not finished until 1480. In 1829, the Minster was in grave danger from fire when one Jonathan Martin, said to be a madman, set alight the wooden choir. A more serious fire broke out on 2 May 1840 which destroyed a large section of the south-west tower. Fire has been a recurrent threat to the Minster at York.

The incident in 1829 involving Jonathan Martin was described in contemporary accounts as follows. Martin was 'a religious fanatic' who came from Hexham in Northumberland. In his early life he was apprenticed as a tanner and he also spent some time at sea, 'where his skull was fractured'. For several years he had made his living through selling a pamphlet giving 'a narrative of his life'. Martin alleged that he had been prompted to set fire to the Minster by two dreams. He had hidden himself in the Minster after attending services on Sunday 1 February and climbed into the choir using a rope cut 'from the prayer bell' in the belfry. He made a pile of cushions, books, surplices, upholstery torn from the furniture, and set two fires, one near the archbishop's throne, and the other near the organ. He then escaped by breaking one of the windows, taking with him 'the gold fringe from the pulpit, velvet from the archbishop's throne, and a small Bible':

A panoramic view of the old part of York with the cluster of buildings forming an interesting foreground to the Minster. (P. Acomb)

The fire was discovered about seven o'clock in the morning by one of the choristers, a lad named Swinbank, who saw smoke issuing through the roof; and although the most prompt assistance was given, the fire raged with great fury for several hours, but it was found impossible to save any part of the woodwork of this noble edifice. The roof caught fire from the organ; and by half-past eleven o'clock, the whole of the beautiful tabernacle work of carved oak, which adorned the prayer-house, the stalls, the pulpit, the cathedra, the fine organ, and the roof, were destroyed; and nothing remained but a mass of burning ruins, which covered the floor, and transformed this part of the cathedral into a vast ignited furnace.

The investigation into the causes of the fire 'fixed the guilt so clearly on Martin that a reward of £100 was offered for his apprehension.' He was soon captured at the home of a relative near Hexham and was tried at the next assizes in York 'before Mr. Baron Hullock'. After a trial lasting about nine hours, he was acquitted on the ground of insanity. He was 'ordered to be confined in St Luke's hospital, London', where he later died in 1838. The damage done by the fire was estimated at £70,000, nearly all of which was raised by public subscription. The Minster was reopened for services on 6 May 1832.

York celebrated the 500th anniversary of the consecration of the Minster in 1972. This celebration was only made possible by the very latest techniques in building and construction, for, in April 1967, it was announced that the Minster could fall down within the space of fifteen years unless a major restoration programme was started almost immediately. Huge cracks had been discovered in the fabric of the building. The towers were found to be bulging outwards and leaning dangerously out of plumb. It would take the sum of £2 million to repair and restore the Minster and prevent a calamitous end to such a fine and beautiful building. Happily, the sum was raised, mainly from industry, commerce and local authorities, but a significant portion also came pouring into the appeal fund from schools, individuals, local parishes and societies. Overseas visitors and tourists also contributed significantly to the fund.

The Minster is remarkable, not only as the largest cathedral in England, but especially for the magnificent East Window, which contains 2,000 square feet of glass and is the largest stained-glass window in the world. The medieval Five Sisters window in the north transept is made up of grisaille glass panels, and is one of the finest such specimens still extant. In all, almost one half of all the medieval glass in England is to be found in the Minster. To save the glass alone was a splendid achievement, but to save and restore the Minster as a whole, and in only five years, was a feat of modern engineering that will long be remembered.

Fire was yet again to prove a major problem for the Minster in July 1984. The Minster came very close to much more serious damage than the roof burning down. The famous and irreplaceable Rose Window, built in Tudor times, was almost completely lost. Fire broke out early in the morning of 9 July 1984 in the south transept. The cause of the fire was most likely a lightning strike, which hit the roof of the cathedral some time shortly after midnight. The local area had been experiencing very hot weather and a typical summer electrical storm had broken out over the plain of York. Fire alarms in the Minster were not immediately activated, probably as a result of the electrical damage caused by the bolt of lightning. However, criticisms were later made by the official enquiry into the cause of the blaze that the fire detection system was inadequate and perhaps faulty.

By the time the fire was discovered, the flames were well established in the dry oak beams of the roof. The lead covering on the roof made it almost impossible to tackle the fire effectively. Around 150 fire fighters from North Yorkshire took over two hours to bring the fire under control. The roof collapsed at about 4.00 a.m. This made it easier for the fire fighters to deal with the flames directly and the burning timbers as they fell to the floor.

The sixteenth-century Rose Window was badly damaged in the fire. The original Tudor glass had cracked, and the lead and solder frames for the stained glass had melted. It was estimated at the time that the glass had cracked into around 40,000 pieces. The Rose Window was eventually restored through a process that involved sticking clear plastic on the outside of the seventy-three separate glass panels that made up the window. Later, a specially designed adhesive was used to sandwich the original glass pieces between two layers of clear glass. This process was described by the restorer as being 'rather like making a Tudor glass sandwich.' In total the Rose Window has over 8,000 individual pieces of glass. It was only possible to restore the fire damage successfully because of the high quality of maintenance work that was previously done on the windows and the medieval glass in the late 1960s. On 4 November 1988, a commemorative service, attended by the Queen, marked the successful completion of the restoration of the Minster.

Space does not allow here for further description of the Minster, nor indeed of the many other historic aspects, facets and memorable buildings of the city of York. The Guildhall, the Merchant Adventurers' Hall, the museums in the castle and St Mary's Abbey, the many medieval churches, the narrow streets (particularly the Shambles) to name but a few examples, warrant further investigation in their own right. However, as with most historical sites and monuments, the delights of York are best experienced by personal visits and discovery. York is fortunate in having so much to see and experience that even the most frequent visitor cannot claim to have seen it all. The city of York has something to offer for all and it only remains for us to take advantage of its many gifts and charms.

Chapter Seven

Robin Hood of Yorkshire

Of all the characters and personalities in popular English legend and folklore, perhaps none is better known and loved than Robin Hood. The tales of his exploits have long been favourites since medieval times. As a champion of truth and right, redresser of evils and protector of the poor and oppressed, Robin Hood has achieved immortality in legend, fable, verse and song. Much embellishment and romantic fiction has been added to the true history of Robin Hood over the centuries, but there is ample evidence to show that he was a real person and not a popular myth. As to exactly who he was, there is some controversy; and opinions vary as to his true identity.

Some say that he was the Earl of Fitzwarren in King John's time. Many of the ballads claim that Robin was the rightful Earl of Huntingdon. These two claims are the most established possible origins of the famous outlaw. However, there is a great deal of documented evidence to support the claim that Robin Hood was in fact born in Yorkshire, at Wakefield or thereabouts, in or around the year 1290.

Yorkshire's claim to the famous outlaw does not rest solely in the fact of his birthplace. Many other events and escapades in his life are centred in the county. In spite of the popular tradition that he was born and bred in Nottingham, the Court Rolls of the Manor of Wakefield tell of one Robert Hood during the reign of Edward II. This Robert Hood and his wife Matilda are mentioned on a number of occasions in the Court Rolls. In particular, the forfeiture of their house is noted after Robert Hood was outlawed. He appears to have been a follower of the Earl of Lancaster in a rebellion against the King, and was declared an outlaw after the rebels' defeat at the battle of Boroughbridge in 1322. From then on he is said to have changed his name to Robin Hood, and his wife's name to Maid Marian, and taken to the 'greenwood', or the open countryside and forest.

Popular legend tells of his life in Sherwood Forest, but this simply means the 'shire-wood' at which the boundaries of the three shires meet. The 'shire-wood' was a vast forest that stretched from Nottinghamshire in the south, to Wensleydale and Teesdale in the north, and the Yorkshire coast to the east. Part of this 'shire-wood' forest, known as Barnsdale, situated in the West Riding of Yorkshire, is closely associated with numerous episodes in the outlaw's life. John Leland wrote of Barnsdale, in the time of Henry VIII, as follows: 'Between Milbourne and Ferrybridge, I saw the wood and famous forest of Barnsdale, where they say that Robin Hood lived like an outlaw.' Other mentions of Barnsdale Forest can be found in the many ballads and folk tales about Robin Hood. These ballads also provide supporting evidence of Robin Hood's other connections with Yorkshire.

One of the most famous of these ballads tells of the fight between Robin Hood and the Pinder of Wakefield. The Pinder was a man called George-a-Green and it was his duty to take care of stray cattle and other wandering animals and keep them in a pinfold or pound. So the Pinder performed the role of a sort of local or rural policeman and warden, long before such posts were commonly regularised by towns or village communities. Apparently, Robin and two other outlaws were once caught and thrashed by the Pinder for walking through a field of corn.

The verse ballad describing these incidents states:

> In Wakefield there lives a jolly Pinder,
> In Wakefield all on a green,
> There is neither knight nor squire, said the Pinder,
> Nor Baron that is so bold,
> Dare make a trespass to the town of Wakefield
> But his pledge goes to the Pinfold.

Later in the ballad we learn that the Pinder and the outlaws:

> fought on for a long summer's day,
> till that their swords on their broad bucklers,
> were broke fast into their hands.

The Pinder is then invited by Robin to join the outlaw band:

> And wilt thou forsake the Pinder, his craft,
> And go to the greenwood with me,
> Thou shalt have a livery twice every year,
> One green and the other brown.

The New Inn and the Robin Hood Inn, Robin Hood's Well.

Of all the ballads concerning Robin Hood and his outlaws, the oldest extant example is *The Lytell Geste of Robin* Hood, published in 1489. The *Lytell Geste* is divided into eight 'fyttes', or parts, and in this epic ballad many of the adventures of the outlaw are first told. For example, the third 'fytte' tells of an encounter with the Sheriff of Nottingham. The fifth 'fytte' tells of an archery match at Nottingham. Other parts of the ballad reaffirm Robin's connections with the county of Yorkshire, and tell of Robin and the Monks of St Mary's Abbey, York, and of other locations in the county.

Another of the famous stories of the escapades of Robin Hood tells of the meeting with the 'curtal Friar', or Friar Tuck as he is more commonly known. Robin meets Friar Tuck in the woods and compels the Friar to carry him over the River Skell.

> And coming to the Fountain Dale,
> No further would he ride.
> There he was aware of a curtal Friar,
> Walking by the waterside.
> The Friar had on a harness good,
> And on his head a cap of steel,
> Broad sword and buckler by his side,
> And they became him well.
> The curtal Friar had kept Fountain Dale,
> Seven long years and more.
> There was neither knight, lord, not Earl,
> Could make him yield before.

Robin is carried across the river and, in his turn, carries the Friar back. Then Robin, after threatening the Friar, is carried over a second time. On reaching the middle of the river, Robin is thrown into the water by the monk. Following this insult, Robin takes his sword and challenges the Friar. In the ensuing fight, Robin is beaten back by the Friar and is only saved by the timely intervention of the other outlaws, Little John and Will Scarlet. Further legends tell that the Friar joins the outlaws.

Although many of the outlaw's exploits are set in Sherwood Forest and Nottinghamshire, some of the early ballads describe Robin's departure from there after several serious attempts by the King's men to capture him and his band of outlaws.

> Then said Little John, 'tis time to be gone,
> And that to another place:
> Then away they went from merry Sherwood,
> And into Yorkshire they did hie.

The parts of Yorkshire they retreated to are the Hambleton Hills and the Moors of Fylingdales. During their sojourn on the Yorkshire coast, one legend tells that Robin Hood became a fisherman at Scarborough. On the occasion of an attack by a French warship, Robin turns from outlaw to pirate and kills the crew of the enemy vessel with arrows despatched from his longbow. On capturing the ship, Robin finds 'twelve thousand pounds of money bright' with which he endows a seaman's hospital.

Much closer associations with Yorkshire and the West Riding are to be found in the stories and accounts of the death of Robin Hood. One tradition says that Robin is severely wounded in a battle with the King's men near Wakefield, whereas other sources say that Robin is merely taken very ill. Whichever story is taken, Robin turns for help to a cousin who was the Prioress at Kirklees Nunnery. The Prioress is asked by the outlaws to cure Robin by bleeding him, but she betrays him and locks him in his sickroom, leaving him to bleed to death. Robin, desperately weak, summons his outlaws with a feeble blast on his hunting-horn. His final command to them is to bury him where the arrow lands, which he fires out of the sickroom window from his deathbed.

In *Britannia*, first published in 1586 and translated into English in 1610, William Camden records that Robin Hood's tomb is to be found near the Priory of Kirklees. Many other works also describe the grave and its location. At one time the gravestone was believed to have magical properties, and people removed pieces and chips from it as a supposed cure for toothache. The tomb was removed on a number of different occasions for various reasons. The epitaph on Robin Hood's tombstone is given in many of the ballads and legends as follows:

> Robert, Earl of Huntingdon, lies here his labour being done;
> No archer like him was so good, his wildness called him Robin Hood.
> For thirteen years and somewhat more, these northern parts he vexed sore,
> Such outlaws as he and his men, may England never know again.

Subsequently, a memorial was erected to mark the believed burial place. An inscription on the memorial read: 'Robert, Earl of Huntingdon, was buried here that people called Robin Hood', and the date 1247 was given. If the evidence of the *Lytell Geste* and the Wakefield Manorial Court Rolls are considered, the year of Robin Hood's death was in fact 1347, and his origin is given as the son of Adam Hood, a forester. Other sources maintain that, although the site of Robin Hood's tomb at Kirklees is recognised and accepted, 'whether he was of noble parentage, or an outlaw of humbler birth is not equally clear'.

Robin Hood is described in one historical record as: 'a forester as good as ever drew a bow in the merrie greenwood.' He was allegedly a thoroughly brave and generous man. Although he was an outlaw:

> …he was no lover of blood; nay, he delighted in sparing those who sought his own life when they fell into his power; and he was beyond all examples even of knighthood, tender and thoughtful about women. Next to the ladies, he loved the yeomanry of England; he molested no hind at the plough, no thresher in the barn, no shepherd with his flocks; he was the friend and protector of the husbandman and the hind, and woe to the priest who fleeced or the noble that oppressed them.

The claim that England's famous outlaw was a native Yorkshireman, named Robert Hood, is very strongly upheld by documentary evidence and by oral ballad tradition. Undoubtedly, Robin Hood has far too many connections with the county of Yorkshire for mere coincidence. The origins of Robin Hood will always remain a matter of controversy; that he is one of the best-remembered and well-loved heroes of English legend, however, is beyond any doubt.

Chapter Eight

Yorkshire Folklore

In common with many other areas, the county of Yorkshire is fortunate in being able to boast its own distinctive system of folklore. This folklore is expressed in the many traditions and customs that make up much of our present and contemporary beliefs, superstitions, character and habits. Tales of strange happenings, unusual events, peculiar circumstances, tales both macabre and humorous, are the very stories and illustrations that grew with their telling to become what we now term folklore or legend. This heritage of folklore often owes its origins to customs and beliefs that have long since disappeared, but the practices or superstitions still survive today, even though the reasons behind them may have been long forgotten. As might be expected from a much simpler and naïve past, these customs and beliefs often surround quite ordinary events and occurrences. For example, an extensive folklore has grown up to accompany all the major events and stages in life, such as birth and death, courtship and marriage, youth and old age, and so on.

Among the wealth of lore and legend to do with birth, marriage and death are the following customs, beliefs and folk practices. It was considered decidedly unlucky, at one time, to burn the straw mattress on a bed that had been occupied by a mother during confinement until at least a month had elapsed from the birth. Another custom pertaining to childbirth was that of the 'tea-drinking', a custom not confined to Yorkshire but indigenous to the country as a whole. After recovery from childbirth, the mother would invite friends, relatives and neighbours to the house where tea, gin, beer, rum and other refreshments would be plentifully distributed. The evening would be spent in gossip and, before leaving, the guests would all contribute towards the cost. The custom of giving gifts to the new-born infant was originally intended to ensure that the child would want for little in life. The gift of twelve teaspoons, or Apostle spoons, by the child's sponsors or godparents was also intended to bring future wealth and happiness. Another Yorkshire custom was the gift to the child of a little parcel containing a pinch of salt, an egg and a silver coin. The salt was given so that the child may never lack the 'savour of life'; the egg to ensure food, clothing, and shelter; and the coin to ensure that the child should never lack money.

It was generally considered lucky for a child to cry at its baptism. If a child did not cry it was believed to show that the child was too good to live and could not be expected to survive for much longer. Other beliefs maintained that the child's cry signified the driving away of evil spirits by the baptismal water. If more than one child was to be baptised at the same time, it was most important to see that the correct order be followed. Should a boy and girl be christened at the same font, the boy ought to be christened first, otherwise he would go through life beardless, whilst the girl would be embarrassingly hirsute. Moreover, the boy would, in later life, be destined to play second fiddle to his future wife and would 'never be lord in his own house'.

One other curious custom relating to infancy is concerned with the cutting of the young child's fingernails. The baby's or infant's nails should never be cut until he is at least one year old, otherwise the child will grow up to be a thief. 'If needs be, the nails may be bitten off by the mother'; and even when the child has reached its first birthday, care must be taken not to cut the fingernails on Fridays or Sundays, both days being decidedly unlucky.

Matrimony is also the source of much lore and tradition. The custom of throwing a horseshoe or slipper after the bride, as she leaves the family house to go to the church, was believed to bring good luck and prosperity to the newly-wed couple. Even today, the symbol of the horseshoe is still very much in evidence at modern weddings. Other customs and traditions also still remain. The best man, the bridesmaids, the nuptial kiss in the church, the bride's bouquet, and the giving of gloves are all customs of ancient origin and are believed to be relics of Anglo-Saxon, or perhaps Danish (Viking), traces in our present culture. There are other instances of such influences in everyday life. For example, the drinking glasses we use today which we call 'tumblers' are derived from Saxon and Danish drinking cups which were so formed that they would not stand upright, as all the contents were intended to be drunk at one draught.

Death was also well represented by folk customs and traditions. Some people would not allow a dying person to lie on a feather bed since they thought that it increased suffering and pain. There was also a superstition that it was a great misfortune, or even a judgement, not to die in a bed. Another common superstition in the northern counties was that the south side of a church and churchyard is the holiest or most consecrated ground. Consequently, the south side of a graveyard is usually crowded with gravestones and tombs whilst the north side has but few. Another widespread custom is the opening of the door at the time of death in order to facilitate the newly-departed and released soul's departure. Similarly, on the instant of death, any open fire still burning in the house was immediately extinguished. Other customs included the removal of any mirrors or draping them with cloths, or even turning them to face the wall. The custom of giving the dead a 'good funeral', or 'a good wake and send off', is of ancient origin and, traditionally, every sacrifice is made to honour the dead.

It was also a common belief that death could be foretold by a number of omens. One of these omens was hearing a cock-crow at the dead of night. Another was concerned with the flight of a bird down the chimney. The sight of three butterflies flying together was yet another portent of imminent death. By far the most perturbing and disturbing of any of these death warnings was the appearance of a 'waff' or 'wraith'. The wraith, also known as a doppelganger, is a spectral double of a doomed man sent as a death warning. There is a particularly amusing story that tells of the appearance of a 'waff' and is quite illuminating as to the character of the typical native Yorkshireman as he is often portrayed.

There was an old man who used to shop regularly at one particular shop, but he would only buy very small quantities – a half-pennyworth of this and a half-pennyworth of that.

Engraving of a pastoral scene.

Then, one day, all of a sudden, he fell down dead in the middle of the shop. After this the trade at the shop began to slacken off and soon no one would go there at all. The reason for this was that the customers kept seeing the 'waff' of the dead man standing by the counter. The shopkeeper was left with no alternative but to send for the local parson to exorcise the spirit of the dead man. So the parson came and called on the waff to quit the place and return to the spirit world. 'No, no, Parson', replied the waff, 'I don't want to stay here on earth myself but I'm certainly not going to the other place until I get my halfpenny change!'

Another story puts a different complexion on the common people's attitude towards dying and death. An old lady, who was near to death, was visited by a clergyman who asked her if she were quite happy. 'No I'm not', was her reply. 'I know I'm going to die and that I'm going to heaven, but that's what's bothering me. Not going to heaven – I don't mean that – but the music.' Intrigued at this answer, the clergyman asked the old lady to explain.

> Well, you see, I've never learnt music and I know nothing about it all; and if they start me off with either a harp or a dulcimer, once I get to heaven, I shall make nothing but a laughing-stock of myself. Now, if it could be arranged, for me to take care of the angel babies I would be as right as ninepins for I always did get on with children, and I promise never to slap or smack them. Anyway, I know I shall make nothing with a dulcimer.

There were many different ways of forecasting future events and occasions. These divinations and fortune-tellings varied according the event it was wished to foretell. One of the more common attempts to see into the future belonged to young girls who wanted to know who their future husbands would be. One particular device for this prophecy consisted of a Bible, a key and a lady's garter. If a young woman wished to discover the name of her future husband she had to place the key in the Bible, marking the pages of Ruth 1v16–17. The Bible was then closed and bound fast with the woman's garter. The whole parcel was then suspended from a nail by one end of the garter. All that remained was to mention the names of the various male acquaintances of the young girl, who might be expected to be the likely husband. Whichever one it was to be would be marked by the turning of the key.

Belief in such simple devices and omens is not too surprising when it is remembered that belief in witchcraft, spells, charms and the evil eye was also extremely common. These beliefs were widespread throughout the country as well as in Yorkshire. The power of evil was so commonly held that almost every community, no matter its size, had one special female who was generally recognised and believed to be a witch.

To fall under the charm of a witch, to be 'witch-held', was an extremely unpleasant and unfortunate experience. However, to avoid being witch-held, there were a number of remedies that could be adopted. These charms and remedies that were used to counteract the witches' spells varied in style and formula according to the locality. It was well known that witches have an aversion to a stone with a hole through it. If one such stone were hung outside a door, this would go a long way to keeping witches away. An old horseshoe, which has been picked up after being thrown and nailed on the door, has even greater power to bar witches from entering the house. Moreover, if any girl who while still a maiden was so fortunate as to find three horseshoes within any one year, and then threw all three horseshoes over her left shoulder, walked round them three times and was careful to preserve all three, then not only she, but when married, her children also, could never be witch-held.

Other charms to offset the power of witches were far more obscure and involved. One such charm recommended to thwart a witch was 'to tear a piece of cloth from the garment of a man hanging from a gibbet, to cut it into nine pieces, and to burn these pieces at the dead of night with every door and window securely fastened.' This precaution of closing all possible means of entry was to ensure that the witch, whose spell was to be broken, could not enter during the proceedings and upset the intended ceremony. As an alternative to the above charm and remedy, the last words of a man uttered before he was to hanged should be written on nine pieces of paper, a pin stuck through each piece, and then they should be burnt at midnight; again ensuring that all doors and windows are tightly closed.

Of all the witches in the county of Yorkshire, by far the most famous was Mother Shipton, who lived in a cave near Knaresborough. Born Ursula Southeil, she married Toby Shipton, of Shipton, a village near York. She died in 1561 on the very day and also at the very hour that she had earlier foretold. Her last few years had been spent living in a cave overlooking the River Nidd. Mother Shipton, as she was called, is remembered above all for her prophecies and, in particular for her foretelling of the age of railways, cars, aeroplanes, television and radio, and so on.

These events are foretold in a number of verses, which are purported to have been uttered by Mother Shipton almost four and a half centuries ago. For example:

> Carriages without horses shall go,
> And accidents fill the world with woe.
> Around the world thoughts shall fly,
> In the twinkling of an eye.
> Under water men shall walk,
> Shall ride, shall sleep, shall talk.
> In the air men shall be seen,
> In white, in black, in green.
> Iron on water shall float,
> As easily as a wooden boat,
> Gold shall be found and shown,
> In land that's not now known.

The history of witchcraft in Yorkshire includes some incidents and personalities that have more to do with petty criminality and confidence tricksters than any instances of the use of the occult and working of magic. However, there are examples of witchcraft trials and the execution of witches in the county. William Witham, who came from Ledston and died in 1593, was 'popularly supposed to be bewitched to death by one Mary Pannel'. This woman, Mary Pannel, had been long 'celebrated for supposed sorceries'. She was accused of witchcraft, tried and found guilty at York in 1603. She was executed on a hill near Ledston Hall, 'to this day called Mary Pannel Hill'.

These events occurred at the time of Matthew Hopkins, the Witchfinder General. Hopkins and his assistants were regular authorised witch-finders. They would offer to clear any locality of witches for a fee of 20s, 'bringing them to confession and the stake'. The tests for witches included looking for a witch's mark and dragging tied and bound suspects through ponds or rivers – if they sank they were cleared, but if they floated they were guilty. If a woman could not shed tears at command, or if she hesitated at all in reciting the Lord's Prayer, then she was believed to be in league with the evil one. The results of tests such as these were sufficient to be accepted as evidence under the law and the basis for convictions. In 1612, twelve persons were executed in Lancaster for witchcraft; in 1622, six at York; in 1634, seventeen in Lancashire; in 1644, sixteen at Yarmouth; in 1645, fifteen at Chelmsford; and in 1645–46, 120 in Suffolk and Huntingdon.

The case of Mary Bateman, the supposed 'Yorkshire witch', is more of an example of criminal acts, devious practices and the stings and hustles of the practised confidence trickster. Mary Bateman lived in Campfield, Leeds, and appeared before the Leeds magistrates in 1808 accused of 'devilish practices'. She was the daughter of a farmer, named Harker, who owned and worked a smallholding at Aisenby, near Thirsk. Mary was born in 1768. From her childhood and early years, she was said to be addicted to thievery, pilfering and other villainous acts. After a courtship of only three weeks, she married John Bateman in 1792. John Bateman was described as 'an honest, hard working man.' They set up residence together in Leeds where Mary became a self-professed fortune teller. Under this guise of fortune telling, she managed to outwit and swindle the credulous, gullible and unsuspecting neighbours who came to her for 'readings' and advice. Mary was 'always cunning enough to keep out of the reach of law'. During the time she was lodging in High Court Lane in Leeds she stole a watch, a silver spoon, and two guineas from a fellow tenant. After a fire in 1796 in Leeds, Mary obtained a large amount of money and a number of sheets under the pretence of collecting for charity for the genuine sufferers from the blaze. When she lived at the Black Dog Yard, Mary was said to have attracted attention to herself by 'producing an egg on which was inscribed the words 'Christ is coming'. This egg was shown to crowds of visitors 'who paid from a penny to a shilling for the sight'.

In 1803, Mary began to assist and act as a helper to two maiden ladies, named Kitchen, who were drapers in St Peter's Square. The two ladies and their mother, who had 'come from a distance to attend them', suddenly fell ill and died. Mary told the neighbours that they had died from the plague and, in consequence, people avoided the house. It was later supposed that they were all poisoned.

One of Mary's clients, a woman called Judith Cryer, had paid Mary £4, after pawning her bed to raise the money, in order to keep her reprobate son from being hanged. Judith had gone to Mary to have her fortune told, and was assured by Mary that her son would surely end up on the gallows unless she paid Mary to avoid this event taking place. Another client, Mrs Snowden, gave Mary twelve guineas and a silver watch to save her son from a similar fate.

An example of her trickery and guile is shown in the account of the next incident. Mary overheard a gentleman buying a leg of mutton at the Shambles which he wanted to be delivered to his home in Meadow Lane. Mary hurried off to Leeds Bridge to wait for the butcher's boy given the errand of delivering the meat. On seeing the boy, she pretended to be the gentleman's servant and also to be in a great hurry. She scolded the boy for taking so long with the delivery and 'took the mutton by the shank, gave the lad a bump on the back and said she would take it home herself'.

On another occasion, Mary gave a letter to her husband which she said came from Thirsk and stated that his father was dying. John left immediately to pay his last respects to his father. On his arrival at the family home, he found to his astonishment that his father was very well and there were no problems at all. On John's return home, he found that Mary had completely stripped the house and sold all the furniture in it. The list of incidents of her trickery and deceit continued when she cheated and duped her own mother out of £10. Mary's brother was a deserter from the militia. Mary wrote a letter to her mother stating that he had been arrested as a deserter and that £10 would be required for his release. The money was sent by the unsuspecting mother and Mary kept it for herself.

'The crowning crime, however, of this abominable woman was practised on the ill-fated family of William Perigo, a small clothier at Bramley, whose wife Rebecca was supposed to labour under an evil wish.' This happened in 1806. For nine months, Mary (with the help of an imaginary person she called Miss Blythe) kept Perigo and his wife in her clutches and under her spell by raising their hopes and rousing their fears, pretending to release the poor woman from the evil spell under which she was convinced she was suffering. Mary took all the money the couple had (some £70), stripped the house of furniture and then took all their best clothes. When the couple had no more to give and they began demanding the prosperity and happiness that they were promised as the evil spirit was vanquished, Mary decided that she must silence the couple and avoid detection by ending their lives. Under the pretence of administering a charm, Mary gave them poison to mix with their food. Perigo and his wife, believing that the charm would be beneficial for their difficulties, used it in making 'honey and a pudding'. Mrs Perigo died from the poison and Mr Perigo was seriously ill, but he recovered. Realising what Mary had done and finally seeing through all the subterfuges and deceptions she had used, William Perigo took the case before the magistrates at Leeds. Mary was arrested and committed to York for trial.

On 19 March 1809, Mary was tried for the wilful murder of Rebecca Perigo. She was convicted 'on the clearest of evidence', and ordered for execution on the following Monday. Receiving the death sentence, Mary then tried to trick the judge by claiming that she was pregnant. A pregnant woman, more than four and a half months advanced with child, could not be executed until after the birth. The record shows that: 'The judge, at once ordered a jury of twelve married women to be empanelled to ascertain the truth or falsehood of the statement.' Their verdict was that Mary was lying and not pregnant, as her youngest child was only ten months old at the time.

At the appointed time, Mary was executed at York. The account of her life and trial says that, 'She was launched into eternity with a lie upon her lips, having denied her guilt to the last'. After the execution, her body was given to the surgeons at Leeds Infirmary for dissection. This was a common fate for the victims of public execution. There was a general scarcity of bodies and cadavers for use by the medical profession for dissection and for teaching purposes. A mini-industry had developed in grave-robbing and stealing bodies that could be sold for quite high prices to the more unscrupulous medical authorities. Although the exploits of the body-snatchers, or the 'Resurrection men' as they were often termed, are more usually associated with the city of Edinburgh and the notorious villains Burke and Hare, Leeds and other Yorkshire towns had their own equivalents. In Leeds the practice of bodysnatching and grave robbing was popularly known as 'burking'.

Not all of the so-called witches in Yorkshire were as devious or ruthless as Mary Bateman. Others had achieved fame rather than notoriety for their abilities with charms and fortunes. Hannah Green of Yeadon, who died on 10 May 1810, was described as a 'noted sybil' and was known as the 'Lingbob witch'. She had amassed a fortune upwards of £1,000 after forty years' practice in the art of fortune telling.

Much legend and lore is often associated with physical phenomena and natural objects in an attempt to explain away happenings and events that a more simple and unquestioning world could not fully comprehend. There are many other legends which, in like manner, are associated with various places and localities. The rock formation on the Yorkshire coast, named

Filey Brigg, is said in one legend to be formed from the skeleton of a huge dragon. This dragon had once lived in a cave in the cliffs and for many years had terrorised the people living nearby. However, one day while the dragon was sleeping with his head sticking out of his cave in the sun, a group of brave men climbed the cliff above the cave and rolled boulders on top of the head of the sleeping dragon. Thus, they were finally rid of the beast, says the folk tale.

On other occasions, the deeds of Satan have been held responsible for the more unusual and obscure occurrences and artefacts that needed some explanation for their origins. The ancient monolith in the churchyard at Rudston, near Bridlington, was said to have resulted from the work of Satan. The story behind this claim is that the Devil did not approve of the building of Rudston Church, and therefore flung the huge rock monolith as a missile with the intention of destroying both builders and building. However, the stone missed its intended target and still stands as 'a memorial of Satan's thwarted malignance', if the legend is to be believed.

These few examples of lore and legend, folk customs and traditions, are only a small part of the heritage of folklore that still survives in a variety of forms. The significance of these tales, traditions and customs has often been forgotten, since the times to which they referred are now long gone. In order to understand them it is necessary to think back to the past ages and times, which gave rise to the proverbs, sayings, observances, legends and customs, and place them in their true and proper context. Historically, they held far more sway over everyday life than is generally appreciated. Some of the more lasting of these customs and beliefs are still retained in popular superstitions.

Yorkshire folklore grew out of a way of life that had experienced great continuity for centuries. This tradition was broken up to a large extent by the rapid industrialisation and urbanisation of the eighteenth and nineteenth centuries. These changes brought new wealth and new ways of life in their wake, which pushed out the old ways that were soon to be forgotten and, for the most part, henceforth ignored. Of these old ways, some stories, anecdotes, customs and humour have lasted the test of time and, without doubt, these deserve not to be forgotten and overlooked by Yorkshire people. Many of these beliefs are: 'relics of a widely different past, relics of an extensive and deeply-rooted system of mythology which often predates Christianity.' For this reason alone, they are eminently worth rescuing.

Chapter Nine

Ghost Houses of Yorkshire

The county of Yorkshire is fortunate in being able to boast of a large number of very fine stately homes and country houses. A number of these buildings and dwellings come into the category of haunted houses, with considerable variety in the nature and the manner of their hauntings. The spirits of past owners, of dispossessed relatives, victims of murder and other foul deeds, are among the reasons advanced for the visitations and many other strange and macabre incidents reported from the haunted houses of Yorkshire.

Although no attempt is made here to examine the validity of such phenomena that have been alleged and reported, and no explanation offered for these events, a brief account is given of some of the more well-known instances of the haunting of houses in Yorkshire.

Perhaps the most important and notorious of Yorkshire's haunted houses is Burton Agnes Hall, situated in Burton Agnes village, some six miles from Bridlington. The house was built by Sir Henry Griffiths, who began work on the building in 1598 and completed the construction of the Hall in 1610. The famous ghost story of Burton Agnes centres on Anne, one of the daughters of Sir Henry. During the building of the house, Anne Griffiths became very attached to it and made her two sisters, Francis and Catherine, promise that 'even after her death, she be allowed to remain in the building.' On her deathbed, Anne insisted that, although her body be buried elsewhere, her skull be kept in the house that she so dearly loved. She is also quoted as saying:

> Never let it be moved, and make this my last wish known to any who may come into ownership. And know, and let those of future generations know that, if my desire may not be fulfilled, my spirit shall, if it be permitted, render the house uninhabitable for human beings.

Although the sisters agreed to Anne's dying wishes, her corpse was buried whole. Within a matter of few days, the house was turned into a state of chaos. Doors slammed and crashed: screams and groans and wailing noises were heard. The pandemonium rapidly worsened and the sisters were unable to forget the promise they had made. They ordered that Anne's coffin be opened and, following their sister's gruesome wish, they brought their sister's skull into the house. The noise and torment abruptly ceased and the house, once more, assumed a mantle of peace and tranquillity.

Burton Agnes Hall.

Many years later a maidservant doing the cleaning happened to chance upon the skull and threw it away, thinking it was rubbish. However, when the rubbish came to be carted away, as soon as the skull was put on the cart, the horse refused to move. No amount of whipping and cajoling would induce the horse to take away its burden. Only when the maid, remembering the curse of the skull, retrieved it from the rest of the rubbish to be jettisoned, could the horse and cart be moved.

Many other instances have been reported of the ghost of Burton Agnes, who became known as 'Owd Nance', and she is said to haunt one of the bedrooms on the north side of the house. Another body of opinion states that her skull is now bricked up inside the house, above one of the doorways, to prevent 'Owd Nance' having to reappear to ensure that her last wish is kept.

Heath Old Hall, near Wakefield, is another of Yorkshire's famous houses that can lay claim to being haunted. Heath Hall came into the possession of Lady Mary Bolles in 1649, shortly after the Civil War. Lady Mary had left instructions that the room in which she breathed her last should be walled up forever. For a period of over fifty years this wish was observed but then, for some reason, the room was reopened. From then on, the ghost of Lady Mary was seen many times walking in the Hall and upon the stairs in a state of restless agitation. These sightings continued at irregular intervals for a long time afterwards. It is reported that Lady Mary's ceaseless wanderings were finally ended when the ghost was somehow conjured down into a hole in the river nearby, at a place subsequently known as Lady Bolles' pit. There are, however, accounts of further sightings of Lady Mary's ghost, since her supposed capture in the river. One legend has it that she is doomed to wander till eternity since her spirit was released from the room at Heath Hall.

There is a 'ghost room' at Bolling Hall, Bradford, which is named after an apparition that was seen there during the Civil War. In 1643, during the second siege of Bradford, the owner of Bolling Hall, one Richard Tempest, was a supporter of the King, but Bradford stood out for Parliament. The Earl of Newcastle, who was commanding the Royalist troops, decided to stay at Bolling Hall during the siege.

Pity Poor Bradford

On the night before the Royalist troops were to enter Bradford, Newcastle issued orders that everyone found in the town should be killed – including women and children. Newcastle then retired for the night, but his sleep was to prove uneasy and troubled. The ghost of an old woman appeared at the foot of the bed, wringing her hands and crying out 'Pity poor Bradford.' Newcastle was sufficiently moved by this experience that the next morning he changed his orders for the day and, as a result, very few deaths were actually reported for the capture and siege of Bradford.

A second ghostly visitation is reported at Bolling Hall, Bradford. Richard Oastler was a frequent visitor at Bolling when the Walker family owned the house. On the morning of his death, 22 August 1861, the ghost of Oastler appeared before the son of the house who had once told him that he did not believe in life after death. Oastler is reputed to have threatened the young man that, if he did not change his belief, then he would return from the grave to haunt him and provide such proof.

Yorkshire's haunted houses provide a variety of stories such as these. Other examples include the ghost of Cromwell reported at the Manor House, Knaresborough, and numerous appearances of a White Lady whose presence is believed to be an omen of imminent death. Not all of these hauntings are evil or harmful. A number are beneficial and are responsible for the discovery of treasure and wealth. Stories such as these serve to increase the considerable interest in Yorkshire's many fine old houses.

Chapter Ten

Yorkshire Industry

The formative years, in the latter part of the eighteenth century, described as the time of the Industrial Revolution, are the foundation of modern industrial development. The changes that took place were based on the discovery of steam power which could be harnessed to drive machinery and enabled the factory system of manufacture to be introduced. With steam as the motive power, output quickly expanded and, in a very short period of time, the whole scale of industry multiplied beyond bounds.

Yorkshire, particularly the 'West Riding', was extremely well-placed to take advantage of the new techniques and technologies. Already well-established for the iron and wool trades, the West Riding also had ample supplies of coal to fuel the new steam technology. It is not surprising then that the West Riding became one of the chief industrial areas of Britain.

Industry was not new to Yorkshire, but the scale of the operation changed markedly. There were many small woollen mills in the Pennines using waterwheels to provide power. Iron working was similarly placed, with many small forges and workshops around Sheffield using waterwheels for power and charcoal for fuel. The coming of steam power meant that the new factories were built further down the valley nearer the coal supplies. The coal measures in the foothills of the Pennines are near to the surface; but to the east, the coal is overlain by newer rocks, forming what is known as the concealed coalfield. The exposed coalfield lying in the area between Leeds, Bradford and Sheffield was the first to benefit from the factory-based industries.

The increased scale of industry also provided the necessary incentives to develop transport and communications in the eighteenth century. For as long as the woollen industry remained domestic, supplies of wool from the Pennine sheep farms were sufficient to meet the requirements of weavers and clothmakers. The growth of the industry meant that these local supplies became inadequate. The development of canals and roads, and later railways, enabled large quantities of wool to be imported through the port of Hull and, to a lesser extent, Liverpool, whose trade was already swollen with the shipment of cotton.

At first the introduction of machinery into the woollen textile industry met with bitter opposition, especially from the handloom weavers. They considered the use of mechanised looms a threat to their livelihood. Their answer to this threat was for them to join together in secret groups, making oaths to protect their identities, and smash the new machines and burn

Perpetual shearing machine.

down the mills. These men called themselves Luddites, supposedly named after a boy called Ludd who had wrecked a machine in a fit of temper.

Two Yorkshire men from the Colne Valley, Enoch and James Taylor, invented a shearing machine which threw many croppers out of work. The croppers retaliated by using a heavy hammer, also invented by the Taylors, to smash the machines. The hammer became known as the 'Great Enoch' and it is said that the croppers used to claim that, 'as Enoch makes them so Enoch breaks them.'

The Luddites were not the only group to fear the coming of the machine age. In 1793, a mill-owner in Bradford planned to build a steam-powered factory in the city but was dissuaded from doing so by the pressure of local opinion. This opposition was organised by the more wealthy citizens, who were afraid of the potential risks and the smoke and the soot from the chimneys. Such opposition gradually waned and, in 1800, the first steam-driven mill was built in Bradford. Thirty years later, there were thirty-one mills and Bradford's population had increased to 43,000 people. Bradford continued to grow in size during the nineteenth century. Its population was twenty times greater in 1900 than it was in 1800.

The Luddites were responsible for many acts of sabotage in Yorkshire. The new machinery represented a very real threat to the livelihoods of the handloom weavers and other textile workers. The potential of the new machinery to take work and income away from the manual workers and their families can be judged from the following extract. This is taken from the evidence presented by Benjamin Gott, a woollen manufacturer and merchant, to a Parliamentary enquiry in 1800. In his experience, the progress of machinery meant that: 'Fifteen years previously, it would have taken 1,634 persons to do that which was now done by thirty-five individuals in a week.' These figures referred to the processes of scribbling and spinning in wool production. The average wages in the woollen manufacturing at that time were quoted as being as follows:

Men could earn from sixteen to eighteen shillings per week; children could earn three shillings per week; older children, viz., from fourteen to eighteen years of age, from five to six shillings per week; women could earn from five to six shillings per week; and old men from nine to twelve shillings per week.

During the time of the Peninsular War, large numbers of workers found themselves unemployed as the country experienced 'a stagnation of manufacturers' together with high inflation due to shortages in supply of many basic provisions. In Nottingham, at the end of 1811, over 1,000 stocking-frame machines were destroyed by a mob of angry weavers. On 24 March 1812, a body of armed men attacked some textile mills at Rawden, near Leeds, destroying the machinery and cutting the stocks of finished goods to pieces. Shortly afterwards, on 9 April, about 300 men attacked some mills near Wakefield and destroyed valuable machinery and property. The intimidation caused by the mobs increased when they started carrying arms and raided a storehouse of arms belonging to the local militia at Sheffield.

Cartwright's Mill at Liversedge was attacked on 11 April 1812 by a large number of men, some 'armed with pistols, hatchets, bludgeons, and so on.' Mr. Cartwright, the millowner, together with four of his workmen and five soldiers, had locked themselves inside the property, and 'met the assailants with a vigorous and well sustained discharge of musketry.' After a conflict of about twenty minutes, two of the mob were killed and a considerable number were wounded. The bravery displayed by Cartwright was later rewarded by 'subscriptions amounting to upwards of £3,000', which were collected and 'conferred on the gentleman and his family'.

The Luddites then changed their tactics and started to attack the millowners themselves rather than the offending properties and machinery. The first victim selected was William Horsfall, of Marsden, near Huddersfield, described as a 'considerable manufacturer.' On the evening of 28 April, Horsfall was attacked on his way home from market, and shot by two or more of the gang of assassins, and he died two days later.

In response to this outrage, the local magistrates organised a 'vigorous system of policing'. By the end of the year, sixty-six persons had been arrested and sent to the county gaol. They were subsequently tried at York. Eighteen of the prisoners, including three of the gang of murderers of William Horsfall, were capitally convicted, and seventeen were executed on 16 January 1813. Of the others, six were convicted of simple felony, and transported for seven years, and the rest were either freed on bail or acquitted. Commenting on the reasons for, and the causes of these outrages, one observer noted: 'It is singular that the districts in which the riots were carried to the greatest excess, were those in which the want of employment for the working manufacturers had been the least felt.'

Further attacks were still being made on the factories and their machines. For example, a 'gig-mill', at Oatlands and the Hawksworth corn mills, near Otley, were burned down. Dressing shops (one of the final parts of the process of cloth-making) were attacked in Huddersfield, Holmfirth, Horbury and elsewhere. Cloth was also destroyed in the finishing shops at Water Lane in Leeds. The houses of the millowners were also attacked and furniture and windows smashed.

As the woollen industry expanded, different areas of the county began to specialise in various elements and aspects of the trade. For example, the district around Batley and Dewsbury is still known as the Heavy Woollen District. Bradford developed as the centre of the wool combing and worsted trade. Halifax specialised in carpets. Dewsbury concentrated on re-manufactured cloth, called 'shoddy', and the Colne Valley specialised in tweeds.

The growth of the woollen industry and associated trades led to workers leaving the countryside, where employment was generally scarce and wages low. This migration from the rural areas to the towns was to have an enormous impact on social life and living conditions.

The population distribution of the country began to change and become more and more concentrated in the urban, industrial areas. The potential impact can be illustrated by a few examples. Leeds grew in size from 53,000 inhabitants in 1801, as registered in the first official census in Britain, to over 400,000 by 1900. Over the nineteenth century, the overall population of Britain had grown by a factor of almost four, from 10.5 million people in 1801 to 38.2 million in 1901. Leeds had increased by about eight-fold over the same time.

More spectacular yet was the growth of Middlesborough. Little more than a small hamlet in the early 1800s, it grew in size so rapidly that, by 1900, it had a population of over 100,000. The rapid growth of Middlesborough was due to the discovery in 1850 of iron ore in the nearby Cleveland hills. Smelting industries and the production of pig iron quickly developed to take advantage of the local iron ore supplies, and shipbuilding also began on Teesside.

The iron and steel trades had long been established in Yorkshire at Sheffield and the Don valley. Since the Middle Ages, Sheffield had built a reputation for the making of knives and blades. With the introduction of new sources of power in the nineteenth century, the industry developed to make cutlery for the mass market and also to produce the vast quantities of steel, which was used in the heavy engineering industry in Yorkshire in the latter half of the century. The association of the city of Sheffield with the making of fine cutlery, knives and swords is still evident today as the players and fans of Sheffield United FC are still popularly known as the 'Blades'.

The Midland Railway had an important effect on the development of the steel manufacturing trades in Sheffield. In 1862 a contemporary account of the industry in the city of Sheffield stated that:

> The largest development of manufacturing industry in the steel trade is on the line of the Midland Railway, from outside the Wicker Station towards Brightside. The first of these large manufactories erected in this neighbourhood was the Cyclops Iron & Steel Works; and, the building once opened, the advantages of the contiguity to the railway became so obvious that many other large business premises were shortly afterwards erected there. Messrs Spear & Jackson; Pearce, Ward and Co.; John Brown & Co.; Atlas Iron, Steel & Spring Works; Thos Firth & Sons; Norfolk Works; and others. Indeed, the advantages of the locality are so apparent, that all the new steel manufactories are being built in this direction.

Yorkshire industry prospered throughout the nineteenth century, but not without considerable hardships borne by the people, who often lived in appalling conditions in the industrial cities and towns. The insanitary conditions of the streets of Leeds were described in 1840 as: 'more or less deficient in sewerage, unpaved, full of holes ... sometimes rendered untenantable by the overflowing of sewers and other more offensive drains exposed to the public view and never emptied.'

In 1844, Frederich Engels commented in his book *Conditions of the Working Classes in England*:

> The interior of Bradford is as dirty and uncomfortable as Leeds. The older parts of the town are built upon steep hillsides where the streets are narrow and irregular. Heaps of dirt and refuse disfigure the lanes, alleys and courts. The houses are dirty and dilapidated and not fit for

human habitation. Similar conditions are to be found in other towns of the West Riding, such as Huddersfield, Barnsley and Halifax.

It is clear then that Yorkshire's industrial wealth and prosperity in the nineteenth century was not achieved without considerable social and environmental costs. The benefits of that wealth did not accrue equally to all types and classes either. Huge fortunes were made by some: the industrialists, factory owners, merchants and traders. This was at the expense of the less fortunate members of society, those same people whose labour had produced the wealth. It should come as no surprise that this situation would be the seedbed of socialism and generate radical demands for the improvement of the lot of the working classes.

Conditions in the towns did begin to improve towards the end of the century with more effective local government administration. The undoubted pioneer of improvements in local towns and cities was Joseph Chamberlain (1836–1914), who was Lord Mayor of Birmingham between 1873 and 1876. He was largely responsible for introducing slum-clearance schemes, street lighting and pavements, drainage and public sewers, and other radical municipal achievements. Birmingham became known as 'the best governed city in the world'. Other towns and cities learned from this experience and living conditions and the environment in urban areas began to improve, albeit slowly, across the country.

A popular nineteenth-century verse recalls the conditions and character of the Yorkshire towns.

> Bradford for cash,
> Halifax for dash,
> Wakefield for pride and poverty;
> Huddersfield for show,
> Sheffield's what's low,
> Leeds for dirt and vulgarity.

Halifax.

The city of Leeds is also portrayed in a very poor light in the following verse, which was discovered in 1857 as a hand-written epigram on the fly-leaf of an old book.

> The Aire below is doubly dyed and damned;
> The air above, with lurid smoke is crammed;
> The one flows steaming foul as Charon's Styx;
> Its poisonous vapours in the other mix;
> These sable twins, the murky town invest –
> By them the skin's begrimed, the lungs oppressed.
> How dear the penalty thus paid for wealth;
> Obtained through wasted life and broken health:
> The joyful Sabbath comes! That blessed day,
> When all seems happy, and when all seem gay!
> Then toil has ceased, and then both rich and poor,
> Fly off to Harrogate, or Woodhouse Moor.
> The one his villa and a carriage keeps;
> His squalid brother in a garret sleeps,
> High flaunting forest trees, low crouching weeds,
> Can this be Manchester? Or is it Leeds?

Yorkshire's industrial prowess was based on the woollen, coal, iron and steel industries, and was largely located in the West Riding. Although the industrial development provided wealth in the nineteenth century, the picture has changed considerably since then. Yorkshire's traditional and staple industries have often failed to keep pace with changing technology. Foreign competition has also hit hard at Yorkshire's basic industries, especially woollen textiles, engineering and manufacturing. Changes in energy sources and the depletion of resources, together with other domestic and international factors, have seen the decline and disappearance of the coal mining, iron and steel, and much of the light and heavy engineering industries.

Sheffield.

Deindustrialisation of Britain in the 1980s and 1990s has had a disproportionate effect on the county of Yorkshire simply because of the past success and the concentration of industry arising from the previous centuries. Of course, Yorkshire has developed new industries and sources of employment, notably in the service industries, as has the rest of the nation. However, the West Riding of Yorkshire has clearly lost a large part of its former dominance in Britain's industrial wealth. This has created new problems of industrial decline, increasing unemployment, loss of population, old and out-of-date factories and machinery, and the lack of industrial growth. In spite of this, Yorkshire and the West Riding still continue to make a very valuable contribution to the nation's production.

The changing character of the industrial infrastructure of Yorkshire, and the social and living conditions that have resulted, is brilliantly displayed in a number of recent award-winning films. *The Full Monty* deals with the decline of Sheffield from the steel city of the 1960s and '70s; and *Brassed Off* and *Billy Elliott* are largely concerned with the effects of the disappearance of the coal industry in the North of England. The decline of coal is clearly depicted as being the result of political decisions and deliberately engineered by the government of the time and not the outcome of the vicissitudes of foreign competition and industrial stagnation and decay.

Chapter Eleven

Yorkshire Canals and Navigations

Lord Bacon once wrote, 'There be three things which make a nation great and prosperous; a fertile soil, busy workshops, and easy conveyance for men and commodities from one place to another.' The importance of transport in the economy was particularly felt during the early years of the eighteenth century at the birth of the Industrial Revolution. At this time, and even during the heyday of the stagecoach, the roads were quite unable to carry the heavy loads required by the rapidly developing factory-based industries. Often the roads were impassable in the winter months and especially so to wagons with loads of heavy and bulky raw materials. Road travel was also quite expensive in many parts due to the charges levied at turnpikes along the highway. The monies collected as tolls were supposedly used to pay for the upkeep and maintenance of the roads, but the system was not equally applied or successful. Although turnpikes were unpopular, eventually they did some good and managed to reduce some of the hardships and ordeals involved even in short journeys.

Water transport is cheaper, though much slower, than transport on land, and is especially well suited to carrying heavy, bulky cargoes such as coal, iron ore, chemicals, grains and raw wool. It was also ideal for fragile commodities, such as pottery and ceramics, and much early canal development can be attributed to the Potteries and the direct influence of Josiah Wedgwood. Long before canals were introduced into Great Britain, the natural system of transport and communications afforded by the rivers was well-used and much-trafficked. Locks and weirs were often constructed on rivers to improve navigation and the increased depth thus obtained, together with the waterpower gained at weirs for mills, was of great advantage. Previous to this, it was difficult to navigate rivers in dry weather even with diminished cargoes. The effect of providing locks not only improved navigation but also formed natural reservoirs for dry seasons with the creation of the long deep pounds of water required for lockage power between the locks. Improvements to the rivers such as these have a long history since the first Act of Parliament for the improvement of a river was passed for the Thames in the year 1423.

Water transport played a crucial part in the early development of British industry. This was certainly true of Yorkshire and the growth of the West Riding as an industrial area. Many of the early factories and mills were located alongside the rivers and canals to take advantage of the power source. The textile industries also required ample supplies of water for many of their manufacturing processes. But the canals were, above all else, the 'arteries of the Industrial

Revolution' for they were the means by which raw materials were brought to the factories and finished goods were distributed.

Yorkshire was well endowed for the development of the canals, with the natural system of drainage whereby most of the rivers eventually ran into one another, culminating in the mighty Humber. The Humber basin was the key to the county's water transport system because the rivers Aire, Calder, Don, Ouse, Wharfe, Derwent and Hull were all navigable, or could be made so, by large barges for many miles upstream. The addition of canals called 'navigations', across the general line of the rivers in order to link up their navigable parts, made transport by water even easier throughout the shire.

Canal building in England and Wales began between 1750 and 1760. However, it was the 1761 Bridgewater Canal, built by the Duke of Bridgewater with James Brindley as engineer that awakened public interest and began the era of canal building. The advantages of an artificial waterway quite different from a 'cut', which simply improved a natural river, had long been realised on the continent and especially so in France. Once the idea spread to England it was not long before Yorkshire began to exploit its natural water transport system. The growing wealth of her new factories and the woollen industry helped to provide the money and capital to do so. At the same time, a better transportation system was beneficial to the profits and fortunes of industry.

The years between 1760 and 1840 have been described as a period of 'canal mania' and most of Yorkshire's canals were built during this time. This busy period of canal construction was often marred by unfortunate happenings because many of these early ventures were highly speculative. One particular burst of 'mania' in 1791–94, when numerous canal companies were formed, brought ruin and disaster to many rash investors.

The building of these canals required large numbers of workmen who were known as 'navvies', or navigators, because they were engaged in the making of navigations. Remembering that these great works were built with no mechanical aids beyond the pick, shovel and wheelbarrow, one can only marvel at the magnificent achievement of those humble 'navvies'. Many of these 'navvies' were Irish migrants who had left their native rural homeland in search of paid employment.

The canals also provided employment after they were built. Jobs were available for men to handle the barges that sailed on the canals and for lock-keepers, who usually lived in specially built houses alongside the canal and who might be called out to let craft pass through at any hour of the day or night. Other men found work in towing barges along the rivers where the banks were not suitable for making towpaths for horses. More often than not, it was the horse that provided the motive power of canal transport. Work was also available for 'leggers' in the tunnels along the canals. A legger propelled a barge by lying on his back on a board projecting over the side of the deck, pushing with his feet against the roof or the sides of the tunnel.

When the Yorkshire rivers and canals were connected and linked with those of the Midlands and Lancashire, a network of canals was completed that provided cheap transport between the industrial West Riding, the industrial North West, the natural sea ports on both the east and west coasts, and links with the Black Country and the Potteries. There were difficulties to this internal traffic caused by gradient variations and by the length of cross-country journeys, which might involve dealing with a number of different canal companies.

The Pennines proved a difficult problem for the canal engineers, but this was surmounted in 1804 when the first trans-Pennine canal was opened. A second canal was opened shortly afterwards in 1811. The Leeds and Liverpool canal was started in 1770 but was not completed until 1816. Part of this lengthy construction time was due to the large number of locks needed to cross the Pennines. The Huddersfield canal solved the problem of crossing the mountains by means of a tunnel, 5,456 yards long, under Standedge.

The Aire and Calder Navigation was probably the most prosperous of all the inland waterways in the country. The Aire as far as Leeds, and the Calder as far as Wakefield, had been made navigable by the authorisation of an Act of Parliament in 1669. Other Acts of later dates gave additional powers to the Aire and Calder Company for enlarging the canal and for general improvements. The company's original capital of some £150,000 had grown to over £2.75 million by 1891, and the Aire and Calder Company also paid high dividends to its investors and shareholders. In 1743 the dividend was 12 per cent, in 1785 it was 63 per cent, in 1806, 180 per cent, in 1823, 240 per cent – and, at the height of the Navigation's prosperity in the 1830s, 270 per cent. The opulence of the Aire and Calder did much to stimulate further investment in canals in Yorkshire and elsewhere.

With a total length of eighty-five miles, part river and part canal, and including thirty-one locks, the Aire and Calder commences at Goole and terminates at Leeds, at the junction with the Leeds and Liverpool Canal, thus forming a continuous link from the east to the west coasts. At Castleford it has a branch to Wakefield where it joins the Barnsley Canal. The Aire and Calder remained in operation into the 1970s and 1980s, carrying large cargoes of coal and oil for which it was particularly well suited, but even so it is only a shadow of its former self. Recent years have seen additional improvements to the canal system, with the construction of the New Junction Canal and a new inland port at Leeds, opened in 1958, to replace the old staithes or jetties near Leeds Bridge.

Old Leeds Bridge.

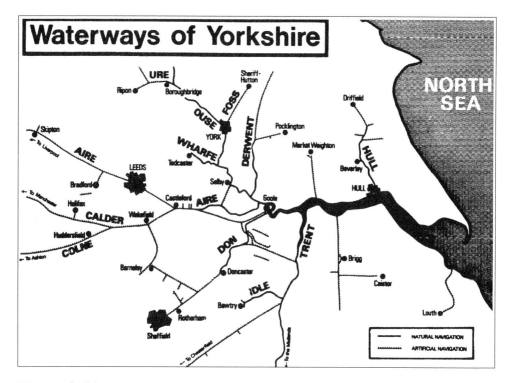

Waterways of Yorkshire.

The Leeds and Liverpool Canal follows the valley of the Aire to Skipton and then crosses into Lancashire near Colne. The Canal was begun in 1770 and connects Leeds and Liverpool and other important towns by a circuitous route of 130 miles, which makes it possible to sail from Hull, via Leeds, Shipley, Keighley, Skipton and Wigan, to the west coast at either Preston or Liverpool. The canal was built according to the principles of the famous engineer, James Brindley. Instead of having his locks distributed along the whole length of the canal, he tried to make long level stretches of canal, with flights of locks leading up or down to the next level stretch. The most famous of these flights of locks may be seen at Bingley, where two such flights of eight locks in all were built. The locks, grouped in a set of three, and a set of five known as the Five Rise Locks, raise the level of the canal by 108ft in a few hundred yards. The pound from Bingley then stretches for sixteen miles at 334ft to Gargrave, which gives a particularly good illustration of Brindley's canal design. The canal is the only Yorkshire-Lancashire canal still usable throughout its entire length. According to a commentator in 1970, 'Most traffic on it today is local, but it is increasingly being used by pleasure-craft and boat enthusiasts who are responsible for a revival of interest in canal and inland waterways.'

By the late nineteenth century, the canals fell into decline, primarily due to competition from the railways which were entering their golden age as transporters of goods. 'Railway mania' replaced 'canal mania' and marked the death knell for the canals, as the passenger train had done for the stagecoach on the roads in the 1840s and 1850s. Some canals never tried to fight the competition from the railways and were abandoned altogether. Others were bought out by the railway companies, either to buy off opposition to the Acts of Parliament which were necessary to enable the railways to buy land, or else to force manufacturers to use rail for transporting goods, letting the canals go to rack and ruin. An observer in the 1890s wrote that, 'the maintenance of railway-owned navigations is often much neglected and generally they are useless for the purpose of active competition.'

The motor lorry in the twentieth century almost dealt the final blow to the canals of Yorkshire. The last boat passed through Standedge Tunnel in 1921, and the last one passed through the Dearne and Dove canal in 1934. The Rochdale canal was largely abandoned in 1952. Nationalisation of canals and inland waterways on 1 January 1948 brought the national system under the control of British Waterways which has made some efforts to maintain and improve existing inland waterways.

The Aire and Calder Navigation remains the chief exception to the tale of the canals' decline and decay, and it managed to retain its coal carrying trade, which was reinforced in later years by the increasing traffic in oil. The comparative ease of traffic, due to the small numbers of locks along its length, keeps the canal quite busy and relatively thriving.

The future of canals in Yorkshire rests on two main factors. The first is the growing popularity of small boats among the population and the demands for the proper maintenance of canals for the recreational purposes of boating and fishing. The second is the realisation that the canals, if properly maintained and modernised, could continue to make an important contribution to the economy. The canals could reduce some of the pressure on the roads by carrying those heavy loads that are suitable for water transport. Bulk goods that do not have to be transported quickly could be taken by canal, as the more recent and continuing use of the Aire and Calder shows.

The canals and navigations already exist and run through the heart of most of Yorkshire's industrial towns and centres. Whether the canals will be revived remains to be seen, but it does seem worthwhile to renovate the existing network to meet future possible recreational demands alone. Any further use of the canals for industrial and commercial purposes would depend upon the competition from the railways and the roads, but there is a strong case for some renewed interest in canals and navigations as a part of any comprehensive national transport plan for the future.

Chapter Twelve

Coaching Days in Yorkshire

Responsibility for maintaining and repairing roads passed to the parish under the Highway Act of 1555. The parishioners were to elect surveyors, whose task it was to supervise their unpaid labour in making roads. These surveyors were also unpaid. This was a very unsatisfactory way of ensuring good roads, as neither the workers nor the surveyors had any specialist knowledge of roadworks. Moreover, the local parishioners objected to working on the roads that they hardly used. Their argument followed the general line that it was the people who used the roads who should have to pay for them. This was to be achieved by the use of turnpikes, introduced in the seventeenth century by a series of Turnpike Acts. A number of local gentlemen were named and appointed as turnpike trustees. The trustees were allowed to erect gates over a stretch of road and to charge travellers a toll for passing through them. All the monies collected were supposed to be used for repairing the highways.

The first Turnpike Act for Yorkshire was passed in 1735, and covered roads from Saddleworth and Halifax over the Pennines into Lancashire. An Act was passed in 1740 to cover the road from Leeds to Selby and, also in the same year, for the road from Elland to Leeds, and the Leeds, Bradford and Halifax road. The York to Leeds road came under a Turnpike Act of 1750, followed in 1751 by another Act for the Harewood, Harrogate to Knaresborough and Boroughbridge road. Then came the Leeds and Skipton turnpike road through Otley in 1754. As far as coaching is concerned, the most important Turnpike Act was the Leeds, Wakefield, Barnsley and Sheffield Act of 1758, which covered the major route between north and south and linked the industrial centres of Yorkshire with London and the South East.

The turnpikes were not accepted meekly by the population, but met with quite considerable resentment, anger and opposition. As far as Yorkshire was concerned, one of the most serious incidents occurred at the Harewood Bridge toll bar on 18 June 1753. An angry mob, mainly from Otley, Yeadon and Leeds, marched on the tollgate at Harewood Bridge, recently erected by Edwin Lascelles Esq., the local landowner. However, when the mob arrived there they found Lascelles waiting for them, together with nearly 300 of his retainers and tenants. After a pitched battle, thirty of the mob were captured, and the rest fled to Leeds where they raised riot in Briggate. The situation deteriorated to such an extent that the army was brought in from York. The soldiers arrested three individuals for offences arising from not paying the tolls. These three men were to be tried at the Old King's Arms in Leeds, where the magistrates and turnpike trustees used to sit. This incident re-fired the anger of the mob. They tried to rescue the captured men and pelted the army men with stones and cobbles. The soldiers eventually opened fire in an attempt to restore order, but this failed. A second volley resulted in the deaths of eight rioters and over forty were seriously wounded. Only then was the disturbance suppressed.

This resistance to turnpikes was to be short-lived, as it became apparent that the roads began to improve and that turnpikes made the construction of new roads possible. It was this improvement in the roads that enabled regular stagecoach services to run between the larger towns and cities. It is easy to forget just how much of an ordeal travelling was in the days prior to the turnpikes and the coaching era.

Ralph Thoresby went from Leeds to York in 1708 and wrote in his diary:

> Preparing for a journey to York. Lord, grant Thy favourable presence from sin and all dangers. We found this way very deep and in some places dangerous for a coach (that we walked on foot) but the Lord preserved us from all evil incidents that we got to our journey's end in safety, blessed be God.

The 'evil incidents', to which Thoresby referred included the possibility that the coach may overturn on the badly drained and rutted roads, might become stuck in the mud and in potholes, or might even be stopped by thieves and highwaymen.

The highwayman enjoys a position of high renown and much admiration and hero-worship. In reality this position is thoroughly undeserved, for the exploits of the 'Knights of the Road' are less daring and spectacular than the stories and myths would suggest. The highwaymen were a product of the coaching era, when travelling was already perilous and arduous. They were a development of the outlaws, brigands, and footpads of earlier days, and became a very serious threat to the travellers on the Mails, Flys and Expresses, and other coach services.

An old woodcut of a stage-coach journey.

The truth about these romantic heroes is that they were simply murderers, cut-throats and vile criminals, engaged in purely selfish gain and with no regard for others at all. But even so, the traditions of courtesy, bravado and polite consideration still persist. How the 'Knights of the Road' achieved their unwarranted reputation is not clear, especially when it is remembered that at the end of such a career lay the gallows and an ignominious death for most of them. As a popular rhyme of the eighteenth century says:

Oh, there never was a life like the robber's,
So careless and gay and free,
And its end? Why, a cheer from the crowd below,
And a leap from the lifeless tree.

One of the most famous or infamous of the highwaymen was Dick Turpin. Turpin was born in York in 1706, according to one account, and at Thackstead in Essex in another. He was involved in a life of crime, including assault, robbery and murder in Essex and the Home Counties. A reward of £50 was offered by King George for the capture of Turpin and his 'Essex gang'. This was later doubled to £100 after a particularly vicious attack on a wealthy farmer and his family. Some of the gang were arrested, convicted and executed. Turpin escaped capture and joined forces with John King, a famous highwayman. They began to attack and rob travellers on the roads through Epping Forest, where they had a secret hideout.

On 4 May 1737, Turpin murdered a gamekeeper from Epping Forest who had discovered his true identity. Turpin, after evading further attempts to arrest him, shot his accomplice, apparently by accident, and fled to Yorkshire. Under the assumed name of John Palmer, Turpin continued his life of crime as a horse-thief and rustler. He was eventually arrested after a hunting and shooting party for shooting a rooster that belonged to his landlord, and for threatening to shoot the landlord. He was taken into custody in Beverley and then transferred to York Prison as magistrates investigated the suspicious sources of his wealth and the large number of horses he apparently had in his possession. John Palmer wrote to his brother from York Prison asking for help but his brother was too mean to pay for the postage and the letter was returned. By sheer accident, the handwriting was identified by Turpin's former schoolmaster who was then asked to travel to York. The schoolmaster recognised and formally identified John Palmer as Richard Turpin. On 19 April 1739, Turpin was hanged at York for horse stealing. His grave is in the churchyard of St Denys and St George in York.

The legendary ride that Turpin was supposed to have made on his horse Black Bess from London to York was, in all probability, the work of another highwayman called Nevison. 'Swift Nick' Nevison was also executed on the gallows at York. York Castle Museum has on display the leg-irons that were used to imprison him.

The hazards from the highwaymen were by no means the only pitfalls that the travellers would have to contend with. Many roads were impassable for significant periods of time during the winter and, even when it was possible to complete a journey free of natural barriers, it was still necessary to make frequent stops for rests or to change horses.

Ralph Thoresby, elsewhere in his diary, describes another disadvantage of early road transport by coach: 'February 19th 1683 – Up pretty timely preparing for a journey, and somewhat concerned about company and fearful of being confined to the coach for so many days with unsuitable persons.' Also from his diary, it appears to have taken six days to complete the journey from York to London. An early coaching bill of 1706 shows that some little progress had been made in travelling time; the York to London stagecoach advertised on the handbill made the claim that the journey would be completed in only four days, but was also careful to add 'if God permits'.

Once road conditions improved then the speed of coaches could increase. In 1754, a coach with springs was invented which was capable of much higher speeds than previously. The new coach, called 'the Fly', commenced running between Leeds and London in 1768 and actually performed the journey in two and a half days. By 1776 that journey time had been reduced to thirty-nine hours, including stops, the service originating from the Old King's Arms in Leeds. By the year 1780, the speed of the coach service exceeded that of the post. John Palmer, who originated mail coaching, brought about the change from the post to the coach for carrying mails by 1785. It is from this date that the real coaching era can be said to start. Road transport was to maintain its supremacy until about 1840 when the rapid strides in the development of the railways outstripped the roads.

It was on 24 July 1785 that the first Royal Mail coach ran to Yorkshire from London, via Sheffield, Barnsley and Wakefield to Leeds. By the following year, the first mail coach service via the Great North Road was in operation. At the height of the coaching era in 1835, there were over 700 mail coaches in Great Britain and Ireland, whilst the number of stagecoaches had increased in similar proportions. In 1835 the time taken for the journey of 197 miles from London to York was a mere twenty hours, including all stoppages.

New methods of road construction played a large part in increasing the speed of the mails and other coaches. The nineteenth-century road engineers, such as Metcalf McAdam and Telford, were chiefly responsible for the better roads. With well-surfaced roads and newly designed coaches, the coaching era received a significant impetus to set it on its way. As coaching became quicker and cheaper, the facilities provided for the stagecoach also improved.

Stagecoach announcement.

YORK Four Days Stage-Coach.

Begins on Friday the 12th. of April 1706.

ALL that are desirous to pass from London to York, or from York to London, or any other Place on that Road; Let them Repair to the *Black Swan* in *Holborn* in *London*, and to the *Black Swan* in *Coney street* in *York*.

At both which Places, they may be received in a Stage Coach every *Monday, Wednesday* and *Friday,* which performs the whole Journey in Four Days. (if *God permits*.) And sets forth at Five in the Morning.

And returns from *York* to *Stamford* in two days, and from *Stamford* by *Huntington* to *London* in two days more. And the like Stages on their return.

Allowing each Passenger 14l. weight, and all above 3d. a Pound.

Performed By { Benjamin Kingman, Henry Harrison, Walter Baynek,

Also this gives Notice that Newcastle Stage Coach, sets out from York, every Monday, and Friday, and from Newcastle every Monday, and Friday.

Most of the travellers on long journeys by coach were faced, at regular intervals, with stops of some length, while teams of horses and drivers were changed. The coaching inns along all the main routes provided the facilities for this. Some of the coaching inns and hostelries still remain standing, but are often much altered and changed. Very few of them retain the vast amount of stabling that was required by the busy coaching inns found along the main roads and highways. Often the great archway can yet be seen through which the coaches would have entered the inn-yard, a hive of activity as passengers dismounted, and teams and drivers were replaced. The inn-keeper's servants would dash to and fro, seeing to either the needs of the passengers or the horses – for it was a wise landlord who respected both fare-paying passengers and the coach operator's animals. A great deal of money was to be earned by the innkeeper who could match both of these demands. Of the inns themselves, Dr. Johnson said in 1776: 'There is no private house, there is no place, at which people can enjoy themselves so well as at a capital tavern… there is nothing which has yet been contrived by man, by which so much happiness is produced as by a good tavern or inn.'

Only the very wealthy could afford to travel in their own coaches and change horses at inns, which were known as 'posting houses', at the end of each stage of the journey. For those who could not afford to be 'posted' in their own carriages, local coach operators provided the main service, and it was these services that brought most custom to the roadside inns. For these travellers, tickets could be bought for travel inside the coach, or for sitting on the roof, fares being cheaper for the roof. Extra fares were charged for carrying luggage beyond a certain weight. The less fortunate and less well-off travelled by stage wagons, which were much slower and also stopped at wayside ale-houses for refreshments.

Travelling on the coaches and the highways was not without incident, as the following examples show.

On July 1st 1813, the Jubilee coach on leaving Halifax for Leeds was overturned in its descent to the North Bridge, and three persons killed, viz., Joshua Milner, the venerable beadle of Halifax; Mr. John Sykes, an eminent engine builder of Bolton-le-Moors; and David Brotherton, the unfortunate driver of the vehicle. Several others had their limbs broken and were dreadfully bruised. The coach had only commenced running the previous day.

Another fatal coaching accident happened on 28 August 1823.

The Fleece coach, on its road to Sheffield, was overturned at the foot of Shelly Bank, six miles from Huddersfield, owing to the coachman driving at full speed down the hill, without locking the wheel. Amongst the passengers were nine Methodist preachers on their way to a conference at Sheffield. Two of them, the Rev. Mr. Sargent and the Rev. Edward Baker Lloyd, were killed on the spot, and six of the others received either fractures, dislocations or dangerous contusions, from which they ultimately recovered. A verdict of manslaughter was returned against the driver.

Other examples of the dangers of coach travel include the following accounts of some typical accidents:

The True Blue coach, returning from Wakefield to Leeds, on November 22nd 1827, was overturned at Bell-hill, and three persons died by the accident, viz., William Herfield, the driver, killed on the spot, Mr. Charles Cope, of Leeds, and Mr. James Burrell, of Arkendale, who died soon after.

March 13th 1830 – The Manchester and Huddersfield mail was overturned at Longroyd bridge, and the coachman and passengers were precipitated a depth of ten or eleven yards upon some large stones by the River Colne, by which accident Mr. Samuel Statham, of Huddersfield, was killed, and Mr. D. Berry of Almondbury had his leg broken.

On Sunday evening October 7th 1832, the Hark Forward Ilkley and Leeds coach, shortly after it started from the Rose and Crown inn, Ilkley for Leeds, was upset. There were many passengers outside the coach, many of whom received severe contusions, and a poor woman upwards of 60 years of age, named Hannah Allerton, of Farsley, was so severely injured that she died in a few days. The coachman, John Townsend, was said to be in liquor.

The Hero, the Newcastle and Leeds coach was overturned opposite Low Hall, the residence of George Wailes Esq., between Chapeltown and Leeds, by coming in collision with a cart on August 12th 1833. There were two passengers inside and ten outside; but only three of them and the guard (a man called Burgoyne) were seriously injured, namely, Mr. Powell, solicitor of Knaresborough; Mr. Morley of Dishforth; and Mr. John Donkersley of Honley. At the time of the accident the coachman, Sissons, had lost hold of the reins, caused by the pole being snapped in two and he was jerked off the footboard.'

The contribution that travel by coach made to the economic and social development of the nation is by no means slight. For one thing, the growth of the coaching inns improved the standard of service and social life of the community. A busy coaching inn, on a route such as the Great North Road during the years 1815 to 1835, would have provided almost continuous service, day or night, and a good inn's reputation would often be national.

The increasing speed of travel also enabled the developing industrial regions of the north of England, such as the West Riding, Tyneside, Manchester, and the Black Country, came into much closer contact with London. At the same time, London was becoming the trading and financial centre of the British Empire and the rest of world. So the industrialists of the Yorkshire and Lancashire were able to commute regularly to the capital, both for its commercial and social life. Undoubtedly, this had beneficial effects on the new industries as Britain entered an age of wealth and opulence built on the fortunes made during these years of the Industrial Revolution. At the same time, the transport of goods was catered for by the newly constructed canals and inland waterways, which provided the means by which the raw materials and the finished goods for market were shipped around the country. When the railways were developed, such transport of goods, and also of persons, was provided more cheaply and more quickly.

The end of the coaching era, when it came, came quickly. Competition from the railways within a decade reduced the traffic on roads between major cities to a mere shadow of its former self. Some coaches managed to survive for longer periods by providing services to towns that were not yet connected to the railway, but most coaching was reduced to bus services to cities' immediate outlying rural districts. Road transport suffered a serious blow with the advent of steam power and did not recover any of its competitive potential until the invention of the internal combustion engine and the motor car.

It is hard to imagine these days how important the stagecoach was in its heyday. In Yorkshire the two great coaching centres were York and Leeds, with Wakefield, Doncaster and Bawtry also very busy, being situated on the major routes. The busiest year for coaching in Leeds was 1838 when the total number of coaches arriving and leaving on any one day often exceeded 130. The volume of business generated by the coaches in Leeds, as compared with other centres, can be seen in the following figures: 'In June 1838, eight coaches came direct to Leeds from London daily, carrying when full, 32 inside and 68 outside passengers. 1,477 coaches left London daily for all parts of the kingdom. 248 coaches ran out of Manchester to various places; and 154 out of Birmingham.'

These stagecoaches had such magnificent names as the *Cornwallis*, *Celerity*, *Dart*, *Courier*, *Defiance*, *Invincible*, *North Briton*, *Perseverance*, *Rockingham*, *Royal Sovereign*, *Union* and *Wellington*. These names give some clues as to the character of the coaching age, which was sorely missed in some quarters. For example, the London and Newcastle coach, the Wellington, would have paid over £1,000 in toll duties and fees in its busier years. The loss of this revenue did not help the roads in their attempts to hold their own against steam. The Wellington was one of the first and oldest coaches in service on the road in Yorkshire and, it remained as the last regular coach on the Great North Road, but even the Wellington could not survive indefinitely. Passengers grew scarcer and scarcer, until the day when it left Newcastle heading south with no passengers. It left Darlington empty and Thirsk empty. Its proprietors, seeing that its end had come, withdrew the service.

For the last word on the road and rail debate, an observer wrote in 1899:

When we compare the travelling of today with that of half a century ago, the miseries and hardships of a long journey, say due north, over Shap Fells, outside a stagecoach, in the depth of winter, the whirling snow falling thick upon you, it may contrast badly with the glow and comfort of a Pullman car, but there are few among us but would enjoy one more peep, however brief, at the old coaching days.

Chapter Thirteen

Yorkshire Railways

Yorkshire is in a strong position to claim to be one of the pioneer counties in the development of railways. As far back as 1758 there was a 'tramway', over a mile and a half long, from Middleton Colliery in Leeds to a wharf on the River Aire, near Leeds Bridge. The tramway was designed to carry coal as cheaply as possible from the pithead to the waterside where the coal could be transferred on to barges, as water transport was the only means of carrying heavy, bulky or fragile cargoes at that time. The wagons were pulled along the track by horses, since it was found that loads could be more easily carried using a railed track than by using carts on the road. The track had the advantage of being a permanent way, relatively untroubled by the weather which made ordinary roads impassable for the most part of the year.

The Middleton Railway was also the first to use a stationary steam engine to pull the coal wagons by means of a cable and a revolving drum. This use of the steam engine paved the way for the next step in establishing the railway. It was inevitable that someone would come up with the idea that a locomotive could be developed with a steam engine that not only had the power to move itself but could also pull loads behind it. In 1811, such a locomotive was designed and built in Hunslet by John Blenkinsop. This locomotive, the *Prince Regent*, and its sister engine the *Salamanca*, ran for over twenty years and attracted attention from all over the world. The first trip made by an engine hauling coal took place in June 1812 and it has been said that 'this curious engine, which pulled as many as thirty wagons at a rate of about 3 miles an hour, was propelled by a cogged wheel working on a racked rail.'

A fuller account of the Blenkinsop steam engine is given by a different source as follows:

In 1811 Mr. Blenkinsop of Leeds, constructed a locomotive steam engine, for which he took out a patent. A racked or tooth rail was laid along one side of the road, into which the toothed wheel of his locomotive worked as pinions work into a rack. The boiler of his engine was supported by a carriage with four wheels without teeth, and rested immediately upon the axles. The wheels were entirely independent of the working parts of the engine, and therefore merely supported its weight on the rails, the progress being effected by means of the cogged wheel working into the cogged rail. Mr. Blenkinsop's engines began running on the railway extending to the Middleton collieries to the town of Leeds, a distance of about three miles and

a half, on the 12th of August 1812. They continued for many years to be one of the principal curiosities of the neighbourhood, and were visited by strangers from all parts … In the year 1816, the grand duke Nicholas (afterwards Emperor) of Russia, observed the workings of Blenkinsop's locomotive with curious interest and expressions of no slight admiration. An engine dragged behind it as many as thirty coal waggons at a speed of about three miles and a quarter per hour.

Among those who came to see Blenkinsop's engine was George Stephenson who designed the *Rocket* and later became known as 'the father of the railways.' The Stockton and Darlington Railway, with Stephenson as engineer, was opened in 1825 and was intended to improve the communications between the nearby mining towns and the port of Stockton. The railway carried both freight and passengers. In 1830 the Liverpool to Manchester line was opened using Stephenson's *Rocket* locomotive. The immediate success of this line heralded the beginning of the railway age.

Once the validity and profitability of the railways was proven beyond doubt, Yorkshire businessmen and merchants were quick to start planning new lines. The first line to be opened in Yorkshire was the track from Leeds to Selby in 1834, a distance of nineteen miles. There was only one regular train a day which left Marsh Lane at 6.30 a.m., returning from Selby on the arrival of the Steam Packet from Hull. The times of other trains were so various that statements and amendments were published from time to time at the company's depot. This line was extended to the port of Hull in 1840, when the Hull and Selby Railway was formed.

By 1841 the country was gripped by 'railway mania'. New lines were being opened all over the land as soon as permission could be obtained by Act of Parliament and the money found to finance the venture. The 'Great North of England' line was begun at this time, as part of the railway link between London and Edinburgh, from York to Darlington. The York & North Midland Railway in 1839 had completed a connection with the Leeds and Selby line. Further links were promoted to connect with the Midlands line and eventually to London. A station was built in York in 1841 and the city very quickly became an important centre for the rapidly expanding network of railways.

By about 1845 railway mania was at its height in the capital of London, and in the cities of Liverpool, Leeds and Manchester.

In these four great markets, millions of money were turned over almost daily, and all ranks of people, hardly excepting the operative class, partook in the speculative feeling. Leeds was the leading share market for Yorkshire, and the operations there had a considerable influence on the movements in Lancashire. In July 1845, Leeds was said to have had at least 120 stock and share brokers, on and off the exchanges. The streets about the three stock exchanges were at times thronged with anxious spectators and brokers. It was not an uncommon thing for 100,000 railway shares to be sold in one day in the Leeds share market. Early in August, in consequence of the amalgamation of several of the West Riding railway companies, and a sudden and extraordinary advance in the price of shares, great embarrassment was caused amongst speculators by the absolute inability of vast numbers to fulfil their bargains. Many having sold shares without possessing them, under the impression that they would be able to buy them in at a lower price before the time for delivery. The consequence was that thousands were ruined and scores of thousands suffered a heavy loss. The mania exceeded in its extent and approached in wildness any former instance of popular delusion.

The rise of York as a railway centre was largely due to one man, George Hudson, the 'Railway King'. Hudson was the driving force behind much of the new scheme and it was due to his efforts that the London to Scotland railway line ran via York. Hudson was so successful that he was twice made Lord Mayor of York and his railway empire was the wonder of the time. His ambition, however, was to be the end of him. In 1849 he was forced to leave the country when his companies began to fail and it became known that he had juggled the finances of one company to pay off the debts of another, and had sold the assets of a different company to yet another at considerable profit to himself. The prices of shares in many of the railway companies plummeted and fortunes were lost. Hudson was ruined, and although the railways soon recovered, the Railway King was firmly deposed from his throne.

The many companies that Hudson had established in Yorkshire were amalgamated in the North Eastern Railway in 1854, which was one of the most prosperous and well-managed lines in the country. Although Hudson is criticised for his shady dealings, he was

The first Locomotive.

responsible for laying the foundations of the Yorkshire rail network. One other notable consequence of which was the growth of Scarborough as a holiday resort, as the railway brought the seaside of the east coast into close contact with the industrial areas and a huge potential market.

The early decades of the railways witnessed a number of accidents, as might be expected of a new and largely untried technology. The following incidents give some idea of the problems and dangers faced by passengers using the new form of transport.

On October 20th 1845, a railway engine, which was sent from the Masborough station to assist the mail train on the Midland railway, ran into the latter near Cudworth, thereby causing the death of William Fuller Boteler Esq., of Oulton, near Leeds, one of the Commissioners of the Leeds Bankruptcy court, and serious injury to several other persons. Sergeant Stubbs, one of the Leeds police officers was so seriously injured that he died on November 19th. The coroner's jury subsequently returned a verdict of manslaughter against Joseph Wheatley, the driver of the pilot engine.

Not all railway accidents were the fault of the driver, the state of the tracks, signalling problems, or shortcomings and failings of the railway company. Some accidents were caused by the stupidity or carelessness of the passengers. For example, consider the following incident:

On July 13th 1846, the members of the Leeds Mechanics' Institution had a special excursion to Wentworth Park, the seat of Earl Fitzwilliam. Other institutions had trips on the same day to the same place, so that there were not less than 5,000 persons in the grounds. A serious accident occurred in connection with the excursion from Leeds. Robert Neal, keeper of the tap at the Bull and Mouth hotel, was carelessly standing on the seat and at the end of one of the carriages. When the drag was put on to stop the train, he fell backwards over the carriage and pulled a person named John Salter along with him. They were both killed. Salter was in the employ of Messrs. Gott's, Leeds. On the Sunday following the accident, Neal and Salter were interred in the burial ground of Leeds Parish Church in the presence of a vast concourse of spectators.

In the following year, on 16 September 1847, another rail disaster took place, which may rightly be attributed to a fault of the railway company. A contemporary account describes the incident thus:

A frightful accident took place on the Lancashire and Yorkshire railway, near the Sowerby bridge station, by which Mr. Gillard, connected with the telegraph, and R. Weston Esq., were killed and several other persons were severely injured. The accident was caused by a broken rail throwing the last carriage off the line.

On the night of 5 May 1853, between eleven and twelve o'clock, an engine ran off the York and North Midland line at Brayton, near Selby, causing the deaths of John Thompson, the engine driver and Joseph Sykes, the stoker. The coroner's jury returned a verdict of manslaughter against the directors of the company. The jury declared that they were of the opinion that the accident was caused either by a defect in the engine or the line. Harry Stephen Thompson, George Hick Seymour, and Samuel Priestman, three of the directors of the company, were tried at the York summer assizes for manslaughter, but the jury returned a verdict of not guilty.

The future of the railways, from the 1860s onwards, lay in the large railway companies that amalgamated the many small and local operations. The larger companies introduced integrated services and benefited from the economies of large-scale operation. The North Eastern Railway had taken over fifty-four small rail companies by 1914, as well as owning the docks at Hull.

An Act of 1844 had established a uniform gauge of 4ft 8.5in, and a guaranteed service at a penny per mile, but there was no equivalent uniformity in travelling conditions. The Midland Railway was the first to improve accommodation for passengers, which the other companies were not slow to adopt.

When the Midland opened its own station in London, St Pancras, in 1868, the company decided to build its own route to Scotland. This was finally achieved when the Settle to Carlisle line was opened, running through some of the wildest and bleakest parts of the Pennines. The Settle to Carlisle line is one of the most splendid achievements of the railway era, and is a triumph of Victorian engineering. The track is the highest main line in England, and has some of the best examples of viaducts, tunnels, cuttings and bridges in railway construction. The line is seventy-two miles long, took six years to build and was finished in 1876. It was built solely by manual labour, but not without cost. Many of the railway navvies lost their lives in the construction of the line. There were so many deaths that the Midland paid for an extension and enlargement of the graveyard at the nearby church. While working on the line, the labourers were living in shanty towns in appalling conditions, and working in some of the severest weather conditions imaginable. No wonder then that this railway line was the most expensive in Britain at the time.

The Settle to Carlisle railway line and the Ribblehead viaduct have become even more famous and easily recognised with the dramatic action sequences showing the Hogwart's Express in the Harry Potter films, and especially the incident with the flying car. The line is aptly described as the most scenic railway in Britain. The Ribblehead viaduct is the most impressive feature of all the tunnels, viaducts and landscape along the line. The Ribblehead is built of red bricks, millions and millions of them, with twenty-four arches in its total length of 440yds, and is 104ft high.

The Midland line established Leeds as a prominent railway city. In 1865, the Midland, the North Eastern and London and North Western companies combined to build a new station at Leeds. Bradford was on the Midland route, and the company built Forster Square station, while the Great Northern and Lancashire and Yorkshire railways shared Bradford Exchange station. Sheffield, also on the Midland line, was connected to Manchester through the Woodhead tunnel. Doncaster became established as a centre for railway engineering and locomotive construction, so that Yorkshire was especially well served by rail transport services.

The railway brought many other benefits and effects in its wake, and changed the everyday social and living conditions for the whole population. The railway created the holiday resort, as is evidenced by the growth of Scarborough, Whitby and Bridlington in Yorkshire, and Blackpool in Lancashire. The 'day excursion' or 'day trip' was also a result of the railway, and towns such as Harrogate, Ilkley, Skipton were to gain considerable benefit from the regular influx of visitors and the trade they brought.

The development of the suburbs was another consequence of early Victorian railway expansion, as the middle-classes were enabled to live in the green and pleasant rural areas on the outskirts of the industrial centres. Extensions of the railways into the Dales increased the accessibility of these beautiful places for both daily visitors and those incoming new residents who were wealthy enough to move even further away from the industrial towns.

Further advantages came from the cheap and rapid transport of goods besides those accruing from the improved carrying of passengers. Perhaps the most far reaching of these benefits was the gradual improvement in diets as the rapid transport of foodstuffs enabled the town-dwellers to enjoy fresher farm produce from the market gardening and agricultural areas of the country.

The railways reached their peak in the years immediately prior to the First World War. By 1900, the Victorian railway system was so well developed that it was possible to reach almost any part of the country by train. Furthermore, the steam engine was an accepted part of the countryside and was well used by all sectors of the community. The heyday of steam embodied Britain's industrial greatness and supremacy as the Victorian era came to a close. Although the railway continued to reach new heights of traffic and route mileage until 1914, forces were already at work to replace the steam engine as the prime source of power. The war years did much to foster the growth of the internal combustion engine and the return to road transport. The stranglehold that the railways had on passenger and freight carriage was loosened and steam was never again to achieve its former glory.

In response to the competition from the roads, the railways continued to amalgamate into yet larger groupings in an attempt to reduce costs and improve services. During the First World War, the railways had been operated by the government as one single integrated system. This was no easy task since there were over 23,000 miles of track, operated largely by eleven separate companies. As a result of this experience, the railways were regrouped in 1922 into four territorial regional units: the London and North Eastern Railway (LNER); the London Midland and Scottish Railway (LMS); the Southern Railway, and the Great Western Railway (GWR). The lines in Yorkshire were run by the LNER and LMS companies.

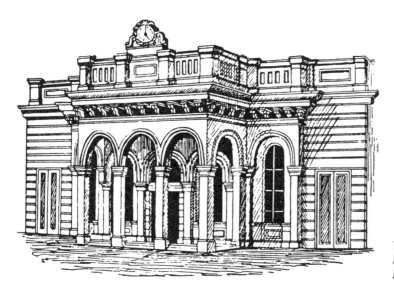

The first Midland Railway station, Bradford.

This regrouping and regionalisation of 1922 did not save the railways and they continued to lose both passenger and freight business to road transport. The expected efficiency and economies from the amalgamations did not materialise. The rail companies failed to replace their traditional methods of operation and also failed to keep pace with the rapid technological improvements in motor vehicles and on the roads.

During the Second World War, the railways were again brought under government control. Undoubtedly, this influenced the incoming Labour Government's decision to nationalise the railways under the Transport Act of 1947. On 1 January 1948, the four existing railway companies became a single state-owned and state-managed concern as British Railways. Modernisation in the 1950s did not prevent the further loss of traffic to the roads.

In response to this, the Beeching Plan in 1963 initiated a major reorganisation of the national railway system. Uneconomic lines were closed, the number of employees reduced, fast inter-city services, freightliners and container trains were introduced, and all the steam engines were replaced by diesel or electric locomotives. The rail network in the mid-1970s consisted of about 12,000 route miles, approximately half of the total it had been in 1914. Freight traffic and passenger traffic continued to decline, and each accounted for a roughly equal share of British Rail's receipts. Over half of the freight, carried in the late 1960s and early 1970s, consisted of coal and coke, with a further fifth of the total being accounted for by iron and steel. Closures and declines in these industries were to have a reciprocal impact on the railways depended upon them for so much business.

Privatisation of the railway companies in the 1980s and 1990s has increased the controversy over the survival and future of the national rail network. The private rail companies were not the panacea that they were presumed to be. Continuing difficulties in operating an efficient, economic national rail system, and a series of catastrophic and damning rail accidents have brought about the re-establishment once more of a nationally managed and more co-ordinated railway service. There have also been some promising developments in the opening of some new local stations, re-opening others that had been closed, and resurrecting some of the local commuter routes in Yorkshire.

Closure of lines in Yorkshire have reduced much of the network in the county to little more than the busy lines between the major cities, while the rural branch lines have in a few instances been taken over by the preservation societies and enthusiasts. These societies are helping to keep steam technology alive in rural Yorkshire and present once more the magic and lasting appeal of the steam train. Societies such as Keighley and Worth Valley Railway, the North Yorkshire Moors, the Yorkshire Dales Railway and the Middleton Railway Trust operate steam services on a regular basis in the county and are preserving much of Yorkshire's considerable railway heritage.

Much could be done with the remnants of the closed branch lines, in the rural and the urban areas. One possibility is to make the abandoned rural railways into country walks and nature trails, especially in the more remote areas, for those who wish to escape the busy and noisy roads. The railway stations and railway furniture and architecture, such as tunnels, signals, bridges, viaducts, and so on, attract many industrial archaeologists, engineers, rail enthusiasts, students, visitors and tourists, to discover and explore the railway age in Yorkshire. The National Railway Museum at York provides much basic information on the history of steam locomotives and the early railways, and helps feed a growing enthusiasm for knowledge of the steam age.

Chapter Fourteen

On being a Yorkshireman:
some thoughts of a tyke in exile

'You can take the man out of Yorkshire, but you can't take Yorkshire out of the man', to paraphrase a well-known and popular saying I've heard many times before. I remember a very popular adage from my childhood that there are more acres in the county of Yorkshire than there are words in the Bible. I was most disappointed to read in my late teens that the county of Devonshire was actually more extensive. (I vaguely recollect this claim that Devon was the largest of the shires was made in a book by W. G. Hoskins, perhaps it was in *Old Devon*, but I'm not entirely sure.) The disappointment that Yorkshire was not the biggest county (and by inference also the greatest) only lasted long enough for the realisation to set in that it would be a very sad person indeed who took on the task of counting up all the words in the Bible.

There is much about the heritage and legacy of Yorkshire that the exiled 'tyke' finds so memorable, even unique, and irreplaceable. For example, consider the following riches that the White Rose County has to offer. The historic splendour and wonders of the city of York immediately spring to mind. Not forgetting many other significant county attributes such as the picturesque and scenic Dales; the bleak moorlands and high uplands; the distinctive geology of the limestone and millstone grit landscapes; the panoramic and stunning views from locations such as Sutton Bank, Ingleborough, Great Whernside, or even the Chevin at Otley; the many castles and the medieval abbeys; the rivers, waterfalls and lakes; the huge variety of coastal scenery from towering cliffs to wide sandy bays and beaches; the agricultural centres and market towns; the spa towns, industrial towns and rural villages; the fine architecture of the proud Victorian city centres; and other urban and pastoral attractions. The list goes on and on. These, and many other features of Yorkshire, make the county beyond comparison. Yorkshire is not known as 'God's own county' by accident. 'You can always tell a Yorkshireman, but you can't tell him much.' (My wife denies this statement vehemently. She says that you can't tell a Yorkshireman anything!)

There is so much more besides location, history and topography that represents the essence of Yorkshire or stays so lastingly in the memory. For example, who could deny the unique taste and texture of Wensleydale cheese (the genuine cheese from the valley of the Ure and Swaledale and not the processed version that is often marketed under the name)? What about the impressive quality of Stones' bitter and Fletcher's bread and cakes, both products from

Sheffield; or Betty's tea rooms and Taylor's tea, from Harrogate (tea now readily available as tea bags, especially the blend made specifically for hard-water areas). Not to mention the other beers and fine ales brewed in Yorkshire, readily available before the mass-marketing of bland products from the huge conglomerate food manufacturing and processing companies. Brews such as Tetley's mild and bitter from Leeds, Sam Smith's and John Smith's from Tadcaster, Bentley's Yorkshire ales, Barnsley Bitter, Theakston's Old Peculier from Masham, and so on. Black Sheep at least continues the tradition of quality real ale brewing in Masham in North Yorkshire, even if the Tetley's and the John Smith's beers and others have gradually become less and less distinctive and less regional in character as part of the generic brands of the gigantic companies who provide for so much of the market these days.

I also remember, with great affection, the soft drinks or 'pop' – lemonade made in the traditional way, dandelion and burdock, ginger beer, orangeade, ice-cream soda, lime and lemon, and other flavours. There were other bottled products, such as the 'non-brewed condiment' white vinegar and a large variety of pickles, which were available via the local home-delivery service of the 'pop' lorry that came by every week from the Crystal Spring. This firm had its main site very close to the historic and quaint Chantry Chapel, which is located on the bridge over the River Calder in Wakefield.

Whenever Yorkshire and food are mentioned together, Yorkshire pudding is inevitably the first subject to be discussed. Even the French who refer, almost scathingly, to the English as 'les rosbifs' have heard of, and are bemused by, the Yorkshire pudding. On one occasion when we were actually hosting a party of visiting French nationals at a typical Sunday lunch (that is, roast beef and all the trimmings) they wanted to know how the Yorkshire pudding was made and cooked, and how it was possible to bake it just so, with a hollow or depression in the centre purposely designed to hold the gravy.

Yorkshire pudding is a serious topic to any native-born Yorkshireman. Tales of the worst experience of Yorkshire pudding will always generate much argument and discussion. The question 'What is the best Yorkshire pudding you've ever tasted?' is even more polemic. For me the answer is easy: my maternal grandmother's, or Nan's, was easily the best. Yorkshire pudding baked in an oblong tin, in a mixture of the roasting meat's juices and beef dripping, and baked very quickly on the range in her kitchen, with the fire banked up as hot as possible. This was then served as a separate first course with gravy, with the stipulation from me that it should be a corner-piece so that two sides of pudding would have the benefit of the rim or crust.

Southerners and Lancastrians, who really should know better, used to claim that this was served first and separately so that not as much meat would be eaten in the next course. The true answer is that there is simply not enough room on the plate for meat and vegetables and Yorkshire pud, unless the Yorkshires were so small that they are not really worth bothering with. The meat, traditionally roast beef but occasionally lamb or pork, would be served as the next course with the vegetables according to whatever was in season and available from granddad's garden or allotment. Finally, for dessert, Nan would produce (but only for the grandchildren, certainly not for the adults) another piece or quarter of freshly-made Yorkshire pudding, to be served with a dribble or ooze of treacle. This was not just any treacle. It had to be Tate & Lyle's Golden Syrup, taken spoonful by sticky spoonful from the green painted tin with the picture of the lion and the distinctive motto 'out of the strong came forth sweetness'. For me, Nan's Yorkshire pudding could not, and never has been, beaten or superseded.

The other alternative for dessert or 'sweet' would be a rice pudding, baked in the fireside oven with the most delicious, creamy and almost burnt skin on top, definitely the best bit of a home-made rice pudding. Another of Nan's food treats, at least was a slab of her own home-baked richly-spiced fruit cake made without any icing, marzipan trimmings or coverings but served with a piece of fresh Wensleydale cheese instead.

Making the Yorkshire pudding is not an issue to be taken lightly in any Yorkshire household, as the following true story shows. Some years ago, friends of ours had bought and moved into a house which was only about two years old, and completely fitted out with an ultra-modern kitchen and bathroom, the latest appliances and all the latest features and design of the time. Within a matter of no more than six months the kitchen in this nearly new house was completely renewed and refitted because the so-called latest design of fan-assisted oven 'could not even bake a decent Yorkshire pudding'. Whatever was wrong with that oven I do not know, but getting a kitchen and an oven that would make a Yorkshire pudding that was fit to be shared with family and guests cost our friends several thousand pounds. So as you can see, Yorkshire pudding is a serious business.

Yorkshire has other culinary delights to offer, the most notable being the cultivated or 'forced' rhubarb from the specialist production and growing areas of East Ardsley, Thorpe, Lofthouse, Morley and Rothwell, an area also known as the 'rhubarb triangle' between the three cities of Wakefield, Bradford and Leeds. There is no other food product quite like rhubarb, in my opinion, and the taste of rhubarb pie, or as a crumble, or just stewed on its own with fresh cream or custard, is impossible to recreate with any substitute. The Spanish have no word for rhubarb, nor any idea of what it is or what it tastes like. The French have a word – *la rhubarbe* – but that does not mean that the fruit is readily available in France. Rhubarb is forced by being grown as shoots from crowns (that is, from the root-mass of the plant) in purpose-built, darkened, low-roofed sheds, over the autumn and winter months, in the total absence of daylight. These sheds are also heated to encourage the rapid growth of the fruit. This forces the shoots to grow in long straight pink-coloured stalks, without very much of the characteristic dark-red and green colouring of the plant when it is grown outdoors. This forcing process also produces more sugar in the stalks, and with much less of the strong acid taste and content of the garden variety (which is far more astringent, and even a laxative). Once tasted, never forgotten. Rhubarb is available in cans, of course, but I do not believe that the tinned variety is a patch on the original in taste, colour or texture.

Rhubarb, because of its very high acid content, was always an important ingredient in the making of jams and preserves. The jam factories of Yorkshire and Lancashire, notably Moorhouse's in Leeds, Hartley's in Liverpool and Robertson's in Manchester, provided another market for farmers and growers of Yorkshire rhubarb, but the premium market was the forced rhubarb intended for the household market. In the 1960s, I remember working in the rhubarb sheds and packing the fruit in long cardboard boxes and, at the end of the day, taking them to the local goods railway depot in time for the daily express goods train for delivery to wholesalers in Covent Garden, London.

The rhubarb was hand-picked by candlelight because the growing sheds were deliberately kept dark and unlighted. It is true that you could even hear the stalks growing in the dark as the leaves unfolded in the plants' urgent thrust upwards searching for any source of light. As a winter or springtime job on the local farms, I quite liked rhubarb picking for, even though the roofs of the sheds were very low and you had to bend very low to pull the stalks out from the plant, at least it was warm and dry. It was less back-breaking work than picking potatoes, which was always available for us teenagers over the October/November half-term school holidays.

One spin-off from the local rhubarb industry was the development of mushroom growing, using the same style and type of sheds, and especially in the off-season for rhubarb. Mushrooms were grown in open wooden boxes, stacked up to the roofs of the sheds, under the same conditions of heated sheds and lack of light. The mushroom spores were seeded in boxes full of well-rotted and well-watered horse manure. The best manure being delivered to the farms in trucks, many of which came from the racing stables and training-yards in North and East Yorkshire or from one of Yorkshire's several racecourses. Before the manure could be packed into the wooden trays and boxes, it had to be mixed with straw and allowed to rot down fully into a fine compost and form a rich and dark earthy mould. The process generated a great deal of heat as the bacteria in the compost broke down the plant material, animal waste and straw. Compost heaps generate much heat in the decomposition process, and spontaneous combustion is always a real threat. Therefore, when the loads of straw and horse manure were being thoroughly mixed by tractors using fork-lift scoops and shovels, someone had to be there all the time with a hose-pipe spraying water on the piles of compost, keeping them continually well-watered.

Not a difficult job for any schoolchild or youth, but not very interesting either (the sheer boredom of the job was always a problem). It could become quite cold with always having water dripping from the end of the hose on one's clothes, and seeping down the arms and sleeves of coats and jumpers, as well as into the tops of one's Wellington boots.

Listening to the radio was a possibility but the noise of the diesel tractors was always loud in the background. The Walkman and personal stereo had not been invented by then, but a pocket transistor and earphones were a possibility. After a few hours doing that job, it was worth buying a pocket transistor radio and you could now afford to, with the added advantage of being able to listen to Jimmy Savile and Radio Luxembourg 208 and the Top Twenty on Sunday evenings. Sir Jimmy Savile DJ, untiring marathon runner and charity worker, star of radio and television, unpaid voluntary porter at Leeds General Infirmary, another example of Yorkshire's famous personalities and, dare one say, eccentrics. Jimmy is also an alumnus of my old school and actually lived in its immediate neighbourhood. We often saw Jimmy's trademark E-type Jaguar car, first in silver and later tartan-coloured, parked just down the road from the school, when he came to Leeds to visit his mother, before they moved to the South Cliff at Scarborough.

It is many years now since I have actually lived in the West Riding of Yorkshire, where I was born and bred. I was schooled in Leeds and, like many of my contemporaries at grammar school, I had to travel long distances everyday to attend school. My daily journey between school and home involved at least two, three or even four buses each way, depending on whether I walked from school to the bus station and saved the bus fare. Other schoolmates commuted daily to Leeds on the train – from as far afield as York, Harrogate, Selby, Hemsworth, Barnsley, Pontefract and Featherstone. Nobody thought twice about the amount of travelling distance and the hours of commuting time involved for schoolchildren from the age of eleven upwards. It was an acquired skill to write homework exercises out neatly, using a fountain pen and permanent black ink for ballpoints – biros were strictly forbidden – while travelling home on the upper deck of the bus. There was always plenty of homework: two to three hours were set as a minimum every schoolday and with double rations on a weekend.

The buses on which I rode would either be from the West Riding Bus Co., or from the West Yorkshire (Woollen District), or even the Yorkshire Traction Co., as well as the Leeds City buses for the ride across the city, depending on the possible routes home. The scholar's permit, the free pass or permit for schoolchildren to use the buses, was only authorised for the West Riding buses. However, the bus drivers and conductors from the other companies (some were one-man buses, usually but not exclusively single-deckers) would often turn a blind eye and let school children use the bus without charge, especially when the weather was bad. The inspectors were a different matter. If one of them caught the bus and started to check tickets the only alternative was to leave the bus at the next stop or simply try and brazen it out and either pretend that the pass had just been lost on the way home, or dig deep and pay the required fare (half-fare, of course – we were all in full-time attendance at school after all!)

Leeds City buses allowed the Leeds schoolchildren to pay half-fares on the buses after the age of fourteen years as long as the pupil had an authorised half-fare permit, which cost a relatively nominal amount to cover the administration charge. This pasteboard child's permit was only available to the children of Leeds Council ratepayers and parents had to apply directly to the bus company for it. Be that as it may, one enterprising member of our class (my good friend Paul from Pontefract, whose father was a lecturer at art college) had a mildly profitable sideline in making almost perfect forgeries of the official pasteboard permits. He was able to do this through having access to the right type of inks, draughtsman's pens and drawing instruments, paper and card, from supplies he found readily available at home. His father had no idea of his son's graphic talents and moderately lucrative pastime and, I suppose you might say, his nefarious and somewhat slightly delinquent activity. The fake permits were never questioned or discovered though they were never examined all that closely. Full fare-free passes and scholar's permits were more problematical to forge since, by the late-1960s, they changed format and required photographs of the holder.

Having so many of the class dependent on the train proved especially useful in the late winter months, when the merest hint of inclement weather, such as ice, mist, fog or snow, gave the school management the ready excuse for granting 'fog leave'. This meant that school finished two hours early for the day, at 2.10 p.m. instead of 4.10 p.m. This was at a time when coal was the major fuel source for many households, factories and industries, and before the Clean Air Acts and growing concerns about air pollution. Sometimes the fogs were genuine 'smogs', especially in the weeks leading up to Christmas, or 'real pea-soupers' as we used to call them. The problem for the school management, staff and the pupils was the threat of long delays or even the withdrawal of some public transport services when the weather turned really foul. On those occasions, the journey home for many could easily become an expedition.

I remember one occasion when the wait at the bus stop for the interminably delayed bus became so long as to be futile, that it was time to cut one's losses and head for the rail station. Luckily enough, this was no hardship for me, for my final bus ride home left from the 'Dark Arches' under Neville Street bridge immediately below Leeds City station at the back of City Square. Trains were less likely to be cancelled by fog; they might be delayed, but they would run, and would get to their destination eventually. How different from rail travel in the UK today, where 'leaves on the line', or 'the wrong kind of snow' or even a relatively tame heatwave can cause absolute chaos to the privatised rail network operators.

Catching the train as far as Wakefield would mean then taking a bus from town, or even a long walk home, but the prospect of remaining stranded in Leeds was far worse. The train for King's Cross was just about to leave from the platform next to the station entrance and the ticket-collector's booth; first stop – Wakefield Westgate. The ticket collector was not much interested in taking my ticket, or even asking me for one, as I explained that I was desperately trying to get home by train and showing my scholar's free pass for the West Riding Bus Co. The fog was so thick that even in the station lights it was not possible to see beyond the length of two railway carriages along the platform. The train left the station almost immediately at little more than walking pace, and slowly accelerated and moved out through Holbeck, Beeston, Hunslet, across the bridge at Elland Road and the Leeds industrial suburbs on the way south. Speed restrictions were clearly being imposed as the train negotiated from one set of signals to the next, with the sound of trackside fog detonators warning of the next junction or potential hazard. After a while, the train came to a halt, obviously not at the next scheduled station stop, which was due at Wakefield Westgate and in normal circumstances a journey of about twenty minutes from Leeds.

Peering into the murky yellow-white gloom through the carriage window at about 4.45 p.m. it was just possible to make out the sign for the East Ardsley halt. The signals and junction were not very far up the line towards Thorpe and Lofthouse. From here the walk home was about two miles, more or less direct across the fields and country lanes, which I knew well even in the thickest fog. Leaving the train, very quietly, though there was no one else in the compartment of the carriage (this was a corridor carriage, second class of course). The guard could have been in quite serious trouble with the company for allowing any passenger to alight from a train at an unscheduled stop. There was no point in drawing attention to myself and getting both the guard and myself into bother. I climbed out and down onto the short platform, as this was only a halt, not a proper station or even meant to be a passenger facility.

I walked past the carriages along to the engine at the front of the train. There to my complete surprise and astonishment, I discovered the reason for the unscheduled stop. The engine was taking on water. It wasn't a diesel or a diesel-electric train as I'd naturally assumed, but a steam locomotive, the *Sir Nigel Gresley*. This locomotive was the same class of engine as the *Mallard* and like that engine held the British Rail speed record for steam of 112 mph for many years. This engine was built in 1937 and is a 4–6–2 LNER A4 Pacific Class, number 4498. The engine was later renumbered 60007 and was saved from being scrapped in 1966 and was bought by a railway preservation trust. The train still runs occasionally on the North Yorkshire Moors railway. This was to be the last time I ever travelled on a steam train, other than on a private steam train belonging to a railway preservation and appreciation society like the Keighley and Worth Valley Railway or on the North Yorkshire Moors or Whitby and Pickering line. I had travelled home on one of the most prestigious and historic of British Railway's locomotives and, even better, for free. By the time I had finally walked home, I wasn't that much later than I would have been on a normal school day. The fog at home was nowhere near as bad as it had been in the centre of Leeds, being out in the countryside and away from lots of factories and household coal fires, so there was no inkling that school had finished two hours early for 'fog leave'.

I have told this story many times to incredulous, sceptical and unbelieving friends who maintain that it can't have been a steam engine and certainly not the *Sir Nigel Gresley*. I swear that it happened, and exactly how I remember it, visualising it now almost in black and white like an old Ealing studios film, with the blackness of a winter's evening and the thickening gloom of a dense and swirling white-yellow fog.

Perhaps you remember as a young child writing your complete name out in full on books, and not stopping with the street and town, or even county, but adding the country, the continent, planet, and even the universe. I recall writing after Yorkshire as my full address, North East England – not just England – and continuing with the United Kingdom of Great Britain and Northern Ireland, Europe, Planet Earth, the Milky Way, the Galaxy (the Western Spiral Arm), the Universe. For me it was always the North East. Not enough simply to be Northerner, and proud of it, but to insist on coming from the North East of England.

I suppose that I've always been a little bit cautious, maybe even suspicious, of the West and the South. I agree wholeheartedly with the views of the poet and writer Simon Armitage, who gave this advice in 1998: 'Always live where the rivers run from left to right, like writing.'

To outsiders the Yorkshireman or tyke is often portrayed as hard, somewhat rough and stubborn. I would say obdurate not stubborn, and resilient just like the millstone grit that comprises much of the Yorkshire landscape. As an economist, I am aware of the dangers of making too many easy or ready generalisations. But that is what the historian does, to generalise from the particular event or incident to a wider context and applicability. The historian looks for the example or individual person or event to illustrate the point and demonstrate the principle or assertion. I tend to see things more simply than that, especially in the case of local history. History is simply the telling of stories. I agree with Peter Ustinov, who said 'the great thing about History is that it is adaptable', and also with Harris, who thinks 'History is too important to be left to the historians.' Thomas Carlyle believed that the history of the world is simply the biographies of great men, which I think says more about Carlyle than it does about history. Henry Ford is reputed to have said that 'History is bunk', but this is also the same man who said of his Model T-Ford 'you can have any colour, as long as it is black'. The great thing about stories is that they grow with the telling, hence the enduring appeal of history. However, we also need to remember that history is always written by the victors.

While researching the extra material and content that I wanted to include for this new revised edition of the book, I came across the following report of an episode that occurred in 1847. The account reads:

January 29th. Great sensation was caused at Wakefield by the suicide of two lovers, named George Hampson, aged 25, and Susan Morton, aged 21. Nothing has since transpired calculated to explain the motive for such a rash act. They were interred in the same grave, in the burial ground of the parish church of that place in the presence of at least 3,000 persons.

If this report is at all true and accurate, then this incident must have caught the interest and genuine concern of the public; 3,000 mourners is a huge crowd of people. This definitely looks like this was an instance of where 'it did come to that, Cynthia'.

My former students would always ask me whenever I set them an essay how long should their answer be. Or they would say: How many pages? How many words? (One was always tempted to reply: How long is a piece of string? Obviously as long as it need be.) My favourite answer, however, was to quote from one of my favourite books, *Alice in Wonderland,* where the King says gravely: 'Begin at the beginning and go on till you come to an end: then stop.' I think I will now follow the King's, and my own, advice.